MW01478002

God Confidence

A Practical Guide for Reaching the Divine Zone

RAY ROBERTS

BALBOA
PRESS
A DIVISION OF HAY HOUSE

Copyright © 2014 Ray Roberts.

All rights reserved. No part of this book may be used or reproduced by any means, graphic, electronic, or mechanical, including photocopying, recording, taping or by any information storage retrieval system without the written permission of the publisher except in the case of brief quotations embodied in critical articles and reviews.

Balboa Press books may be ordered through booksellers or by contacting:

Balboa Press
A Division of Hay House
1663 Liberty Drive
Bloomington, IN 47403
www.balboapress.com
1 (877) 407-4847

Because of the dynamic nature of the Internet, any web addresses or links contained in this book may have changed since publication and may no longer be valid. The views expressed in this work are solely those of the author and do not necessarily reflect the views of the publisher, and the publisher hereby disclaims any responsibility for them.

The author of this book does not dispense medical advice or prescribe the use of any technique as a form of treatment for physical, emotional, or medical problems without the advice of a physician, either directly or indirectly. The intent of the author is only to offer information of a general nature to help you in your quest for emotional and spiritual well-being. In the event you use any of the information in this book for yourself, which is your constitutional right, the author and the publisher assume no responsibility for your actions.

Any people depicted in stock imagery provided by Thinkstock are models, and such images are being used for illustrative purposes only.
Certain stock imagery © Thinkstock.

Printed in the United States of America.

ISBN: 978-1-4525-9697-6 (sc)
ISBN: 978-1-4525-9699-0 (hc)
ISBN: 978-1-4525-9698-3 (e)

Library of Congress Control Number: 2014907763

Balboa Press rev. date: 06/04/2014

To the most significant people in my life:

To my mother, for her strength and wisdom, a wisdom that was well beyond her eighth-grade education and her rural Depression-era upbringing, and a strength that continually demonstrated optimism and God Confidence that is truly heaven-sent.

To my love, Jamie, for her intelligence and drive to explore a spiritual journey, and her desire to find a personal relationship with God.

To my daughters, Paige and Marissa, *you know* and are connected. I pray you will continue to experience God Confidence, particularly when the trials and challenges of the everyday cloud the view of the light. Always remember that the light is shining behind the clouds. Don't ever lose your childlike willingness to be open to spirit. Know that as you move through life you have done it all before. All problems come with built-in solutions—the circumstances may be unique but the ultimate problems are never new. The most important thing is that you are smart and have access to the infinite, where your God Confidence will always have the answer … maybe not what you expect, but know you will always have the answer. And, as you grow, remind yourself that when the world is beating the crap out of you, it is just like a cloudy day, where the sun is still shining right behind the clouds and that *is* where you are too, in the sunshine, in God Confidence.

Contents

Introduction xi

Chapter 1	God Confidence Defined 1
Chapter 2	Only One God.. 9
Chapter 3	Sports as Divine...22
Chapter 4	God Created Bad Drivers 38
Chapter 5	Daily Ways: Practice Is the Key to God Confidence................................49
Chapter 6	Airy-Fairy versus Joe Six-Pack 102
Chapter 7	I Know These Two Guys 110

Conclusion 117
Epilogue.. 121
Final Thoughts...127

Every new beginning comes from some other beginning's end.

—Seneca

Introduction

Wisdom is the principal thing; therefore get wisdom: and with all thy getting get understanding.

—Proverbs 4:7

IN ALL OUR getting we sometimes overlook, undervalue, or underutilize one of the most significant aspects of our daily lives—our personal relationship with God. Whatever our lot in life may be, getting and searching is a huge part of our daily activity. Whether it is searching for the perfect mate, job, house, or wave to surf, we all search. In a runner's world, there is plenty of searching, for the right shoes, the right running partner, and the right pace (comfortable enough to feel like we can go forever, and fast enough that it doesn't take forever to get there). However, much like the perfect pace, finding what we're searching for is really about finding something inside us that feels right. The answer to the perfect pace is how we feel, and the answer to all searching is finding peace within ourselves, which we can *only* accomplish by finding our personal relationship with God.

Jesus said that the "kingdom of heaven is within us," and saints of all religions have made similar observations, noting that peace, ultimate wisdom, and the answer to all questions is within ourselves, through our connection to God. Unfortunately, many have forgotten this ancient wisdom and engage in endless searching in the material world, never finding what they are looking for. This forgetfulness is the root of much suffering in our world, and finding God is the only real solution to it.

However, searching does serve an important purpose in our human existence, because searching can lead to great discovery. Searching and subsequent discovery are at the root of every advancement in humankind. From technology to medicine to philosophy, all the thoughts that produced things and concepts spawned from a searching for something more.

Likewise, our souls are always searching for something more for us, in both the spiritual and material realm. This book aims to provide tools and ways of being that will support our soul on its quest for the next ... whatever it has in store for us. And, on the way to the "next," we may find an extraordinary relationship with God that will in turn be the answer, or provide the answer, to all our searching.

In the course of this dialogue we will explore what it means to live a God Confident life. We will also learn how everyday events are truly mechanisms to our deepening relationship with the infinite. We'll see how specific tools and practices can be implemented to provide direction and action to our relationships and daily lives. We'll find how setting goals, practicing, and trying to get better allow us to turn everyday moments into an extraordinary relationship with God. And we'll discover that all we've been searching for can be—and is—really just living in a deeper personal way that supports our being, allowing us to be a beneficial presence to all those we come in contact with. These are grand ambitions to be sure, but all great discovering starts with lofty dreams, and what could be greater at an individual level than to build the ultimate relationship?

The key to any lasting relationship is an understanding of the real basis of it, and then developing a personal commitment and practice with the goal of always working to make the relationship better. A relationship with God is no different. We may attend some religious events once or twice a week, or once or twice a year (some pastors across the religious spectrum have adopted the title CEO to refer to those twice-a-year folks: Christmas and Easter Only). We may identify ourselves with a particular religious organization, and we may pray/bargain/plead with God. But how often do we pray daily—or multiple times a day? How often do we think about a higher power in all our interactions at work, home, and at church? How often are we in a place of worship but thinking about the pile of work at the office, the argument with the neighbor, or other non-God-related things? Okay, nothing is unrelated to God, but you get the point.

In reality, we spend very little time connected or attempting a connection with God versus the amount of time we spend thinking about other things. Along these lines, Brother Lawrence had many profound insights about the benefits of what he called "practicing the presence of God." On page 43 of *The Practice of the Presence of God*, He observed that

> ...the soul comes to such a knowledge of God that almost all her life is passed in making acts of love and of worship, of contrition and of trust, of thanks, of offering, of petition, and of all virtues; sometimes, indeed, she seems engaged in one unceasing, endless act, for the soul is keeping herself continually in the divine presence.

How often do we treat our personal relationship with God like we treat our personal relationships with coworkers, friends, and family? In all of these human relationships we have particular interactions and communications with each other, rituals we participate in with them, and basic care and feeding of the relationship. But how often do we have a relationship with God where we talk regularly, build time in our day to interact with God and think about the relationship, and do things together?

One quick note: When the word "God" is used in this text; it is my word, my label, that gives meaning to my thought of the Higher Power. As you read, feel free to substitute whatever word or label works for you in your understanding of the divine. It could be God, Allah, Yahweh, the Infinite, Father-Mother-God, Heavenly Father, Spirit, or whatever suits you. For me the label is not important, rather it is the understanding and direct experience of the concept which is the key. The main idea is that there is one singular power and presence in the universe from which all things come. The goal of this book is to help you establish your personal relationship with that power and presence in your daily life.

I am a regular person. I'm not a divine sage, or a spiritual guru, or a gifted seer. I have not experienced a cosmic epiphany or received a message from God. I have not had any life-changing tragedy that has given me unique perspective. I've not recovered from a childhood trauma or addiction or any significant event that sometimes leads to insight beyond the norm. I think that makes me like most.

There is keen understanding that comes from experiencing life-altering occurrences that immediately shift one's state of awareness and being. And while that awareness and being can provide guidance for finding God-enlightenment, I am confident that one does not need to experience this sort of life-altering, immediate event, or any sort of "suffering," to become connected to God. I am confident that the promise of God is for the common folk too. Those folks like me fortunate enough to have the basics of health, family, spirit, job, and ordinary life. I am just living a regular life, trying to find myself and trying to find God.

Sometimes there seems to be an expectation that there must be struggle or some life-altering event to precipitate *the* turning point in one's life. Many times we hear the questions "What was your lowest point?" "What were the times you struggled most?" "What has been the catalyst for your enlightenment/change/etc.?" Or we hear, "At the time it was awful, but I'm so grateful it happened because it allowed me to *x*." Maybe it is a matter of degree, and what some would deem as significant I don't, or perhaps I'm blocking out or waxing nostalgic about truly horrible past events, but I don't think so. And I don't think the majority of folks are in the life-altering event boat.

So what to do? How do we find ourselves and, ultimately, God? How do we establish a personal relationship with God and become able to live our lives in a God Confident way?

We have to learn to adhere to the laws of the universe, and the laws of spirit. Just like criminal and civil law, spiritual laws are written, available to all, and equally applied. Just as with criminal law, if we abide by the rule of law, we have nothing to fear from the police. The same thing is true with universal law: If we abide, we have nothing to fear from the world around us. In fact, we can know that the universe is actually available to watch over us and protect and serve us.

So how do we live in accordance with the universal laws? How do we learn to live with confidence in the laws that protect and serve us? We establish a practice of God Confidence, build a God Confident-life and find our true selves and God, because

- God Confidence = following the laws of the universe;
- following the laws of the universe = fearlessness;
- fearlessness = living in harmony with universe; and
- living in harmony with universe = God Confidence, resulting in a peaceful, easy, harmonious life of fulfillment and increase.

What we will explore in the pages that follow is the process for becoming God Confident without having a transformative experience, a life-altering event, or extreme struggle, as well as the steps to achieving God Confidence. I'm not sure that I have all the answers, but I have found some things that make me feel better and closer to God. These things make me want to know more of God and myself. This will be a discussion of a regular (whatever that may mean or be worth) person's perspective of the divine. It will be a look at the workaday world of job, family, and basic obligations, and how we connect during that normalcy of daily life. Finding God seems easier if we could run off and live in a Tibetan monastery, but that's not really an option—or quite honestly a desire—for most people.

I firmly believe those of us that are in this unextraordinary group of folks, who've not experienced an epiphany of enlightenment or felt the pall of utter hopelessness, are in a fortunate, sweet spot. We are somewhere between the holy and the damned (although I don't believe there are really any in the damned category), and there is always an opportunity to connect to God. Those that might be called damned in some religious traditions are merely disconnected from spirit, and are what I'll call the "available majority." We are in the ever-present ebb and flow of spiritual energy that is the human experience. We all have the call of spirit within us, and at times it is strong—strong enough to move us to action. However, other times it is weak—so weak that we feel alone and abandoned.

So what do we do, what's the alternative? God Confidence! Through God Confidence and development of our relationship and experience of spirit, we learn that this ebb and flow is okay. And despite challenge, we continue to view all circumstances as opportunities to exercise our God Confidence.

1

God Confidence Defined

If you are putting God first in your life, you will not find yourself laboring under undue anxiety about anything.

—Emmet Fox

EVERY MOMENT IS just as it should be, and each is an opportunity to enhance our connection with God.

The process works, and practice will assuredly produce results. What is God Confidence? It is several things, and there are maybe a few that it is not, but I will start with what it is.

God Confidence is faith, but more so it is faith in action, or actionable belief combined with emotion. The definition of faith is "a belief in that which cannot be seen or proven." God Confidence is certainly that, but the context of faith is more a tenet of religious practice rather than a daily or life exercise. The context of faith is one of a regimen or requirement for being a part of something. You believe in God, and therefore you demonstrate your faith by praying and trusting in God and his promise. And while it may be a matter of semantics,

I'd say that God Confidence, or actionable belief combined with emotion, is a step further.

In God Confidence, your actions and emotions are controlled not by the events of the day or by blind trust, but by your personal relationship with God. This is a relationship forged by your internal perspective, and the plan and practice you've established around how you'll live. It is determined by your knowing the laws of the universe and how to apply and abide by them, and thus your emotions are centered in God Confidence.

Furthermore, you believe and exist in an acceptance that all your actions are guided by universal intelligence. You realize that you are a part of that one infinite being, and that your daily actions are in perfect harmony with the universe. These actions, while seemingly nonspiritual, are always, in all ways, connected to and a part of your spiritual being and your human experience. Part of the challenge is that we've always deemed daily life and spiritual life as separate. We work during the week, go to church on Sunday, and nary the two shall meet … while in fact they meet all the time, but we're just not aware of it. Becoming aware of it is how we build a God Confident life. We begin by recognizing, accepting, and running with the idea that we are always connected, and we can do things in our daily lives that support and strengthen the connection with God and all other beings on our planet.

Something to consider in defining God Confidence is *knowing* versus *acting*. We may *know* a lot of things, but we often don't *act* on them. God Confidence means acting with the confidence of knowing, living, and doing in harmony, and in a deliberate and intentional manner. Thus, all of these "knowings" assume action and integration into our daily lives. The following are some examples of God Confident knowings:

Spiritual Knowings

- knowing the power of God is within you
- knowing you are right when you do all things in accordance with spiritual law
- knowing you don't need or want to judge everything and anything
- knowing what a powerful presence you are, just as you are
- knowing everything is and was a thought before it was a thing
- knowing that prayer/meditation/quiet time, or the like, is your time to talk and listen to God
- knowing that any time is your time to talk and listen to God
- knowing that the universe guides you
- knowing that you are a spiritual being always connected to the infinite, despite times when your awareness wanes
- knowing a smile is really one of the greatest gifts you can give to someone—and to yourself
- knowing there is always enough

Personal/Relationship Knowings

- knowing that others can be right, and you can let them be right
- knowing that everyone (including you) always tries their best at this particular moment in time
- knowing that while someone's best may not meet your expectations, you can still accept their actions
- knowing that your responsibilities to others are perfect for you at this point in time
- knowing that you can learn, seek advice, get help; that all are tools for you as you build your life
- knowing it really is your world, and everyone else is just living in it—what kind of world do you want?

- knowing you don't necessarily have to know the reason right now
- knowing that the timing of a circumstance or event is not always reasonable (Why did that have to happen now?), but it always has a reason
- knowing you are okay regardless of the circumstance and despite not knowing what the reason is ("Ours is not to reason why …")
- knowing that acceptance of a thing is not defeat; it is, in fact, a victory
- knowing that you are in control and can choose kindness, love, joy, or humor at any time for any reason, as you are the reason for it all anyway

Activity/Material Knowings

- knowing you're exactly where you need to be at this moment
- knowing you can create your future
- knowing there is always time
- knowing we are all great in our own way, so find your way and relish it
- knowing no one else needs to know what our greatness is
- knowing it is all temporary, and because of this, any time could be our last moment, or our first moment
- knowing that every new beginning is some other beginning's end
- knowing that the more we practice, the better we become—at anything, including spiritual practices
- knowing the timing of the receipt of our desires and intentions is not exclusively ours to define

And finally,

- knowing that you know all of the things above and that you can act like you know them

The context of God Confidence is acting like you truly believe you are in control. There is a bigger presence than you at work, and the activation of that presence is a matter of choice by you. God Confidence is the faith, knowledge, and willingness to live your life by taking action and moving forward based on confidence. As Norman Vincent Peale once said, "Believe in yourself! Have faith in your abilities! Without a humble but reasonable confidence in your own powers, you cannot be successful or happy."

If I believe or have faith in something in the context of God Confidence, this means I'll do things throughout the day that engage, nurture, and support that belief, or more correctly, that feeling. You see, God Confidence is as much feeling, and working with that feeling, as it is anything else. Ester and Jerry Hicks have several books in which they share their conversations with Abraham (a spiritual collective) and note that emotions serve as our internal guidance system. This guidance system lets us know when the things we do and think are in harmony with spirit and bring us greater connection, or when they are out of sorts and disconnect us.

Thus God Confidence requires the action of faith to include a daily practice that includes awareness of our feelings as they are associated with specific actions and thoughts. Since this concept is so important, we will discuss it extensively in the chapters that follow. The rest of this book will focus on being aware of our feelings by understanding what it feels like when we're connected to and in relationship with God. Subsequently, we will explore finding practices to help us reach that feeling more often and also be more able to identify it, practice it, and thus make it a habit that establishes God Confidence.

A number of years ago my wife and I went on a trip to Bali. One day we rented a car and driver to explore the island. Our driver was a kind young gentleman who spoke English and provided us a wonderful tour. He took us to a number of spots, allowing us to stop and explore the temples, shops, and markets, and then took us safely back to the hotel. During our time with him, we were totally engrossed in the adventure of seeing a part of the world we'd never experienced before. We got a feel of the local flair by being guided to points of interest. It was a unique experience of having the chance to enjoy the day without worrying about schedule, where we were, how we were going to get to our next destination (or even what that specifically was), or how we were getting back. For our driver, I'm quite sure this was a routine, that he had regular spots that he took the tourists to, and that maybe there were even under-the-table deals with the woodcarvers and shop owners that he took us to see. Nonetheless, we were confident we were safe. We were getting to venture out a bit while never risking getting lost, as if we'd been on our own, and having some confidence that we were getting to see some measure of the real Bali. We thoroughly enjoyed the ancient temples, woodcarving shops, and village markets.

This guided tour for our day in Bali can be our everyday life with God Confidence. We have a guide each moment of our lives. The guide has the intent to help us experience our lives, enjoy ourselves and our surroundings, and keep us safe. When we live with God Confidence, we know we're being looked after with God as our guide. There is a grand itinerary for the day and for our life. We need not be concerned with the schedule, or how we're getting from point A to B, or even if it is actually point A to D. We simply enjoy, take in the world around us, support those we love, take joy in serving, make ourselves and others laugh, give thanks to others and to God, and stay engrossed in the moment without the past or future distracting us. The thing I remember most clearly about that day is the lack of fear or worry. That is not to say we were careless or oblivious to the goings-on around us, but the focus and attention was on the joy of the experience. I was truly experiencing my self and the activity of that day, not what was next or what had been. That is a liberating and powerful feeling, and we can experience it every day.

Taking a guided tour of Bali allowed us to see things we never would have seen otherwise. It gave us the courage to venture beyond the comforts of the hotel property, and it allowed us to experience that world without having to think in great detail about what to do.

God Confidence provides the ability (opportunity) to stay in the flow and the now by undergirding all our thoughts and actions in peaceful oneness with nature, spirit, and the universe—in God.

So many times we get so caught up in the philosophical questions about how the world works, why things happen, or in our need to find meaning and control that we end up spinning our wheels (replaying the past or the future), and breaking our connection and missing the now. God Confidence allows us to easily and effortlessly accept the world around us without judgment and struggle on how to explain it.

God Confidence means that even though things can happen (which they obviously do), you can know at your God level (or core self) that they are a part of you, your life, your essence, and your journey, and they need no explanation. There is not a desire to figure out what the message is, what the meaning is, or what you are to learn. With God Confidence, you simply encounter the event and continue on with gratitude and knowledge. Without this peace, one can spend a great deal of time struggling to find the meaning in life events, and the explanation of why people behave as they do. However, I've rarely heard anyone come up with a reason or explanation that makes the situation any better, or provides the person with any direction about how to do things differently in the future.

In most instances, all we experience is judgment about the event or people involved. This can turn into "analysis paralysis" as we wrestle with the not knowing and the inexplicability of certain happenings. We paralyze ourselves as we replay how events may have gone differently if only we would have said something different or if the other person would have responded differently, or if the timing would have been different—or a host of ifs, ands, buts, and ors. All the while the world around us is going by, and we've missed another sunrise or any number of special yet fleeting moments. Don't miss anything else! Live with the utmost care for yourself. Live with the keenest awareness of being a part of something larger, and the knowledge of the opportunity, joy, and gratitude that is in every moment. Live in God Confidence.

2
Only One God

Too many religions but only one god, I don't need another savior ...

—"I Don't Wanna Stop," Ozzy Osbourne

THE OZ MAN cometh, and he bringeth the truth.

Part of the modern challenge with establishing a relationship with God is our need to identify people and things with simple labels. This is so that we don't really have to understand a person or a thing, we just have to label them, and that tells us all we need to know. But that shortcut, while sometimes useful, too often crowds out someone's true essence. We've come to expect that one must identify oneself with a particular religion to be considered religious/spiritual/chosen.

However, I find that religious doctrine and dogma is not required to be spiritual and God Confident. Many (including Ozzy) argue, and I agree, that there is but one God, just with different names and different paths all leading to the same ultimate.

I have taken elements from a number of sources to establish my spiritual beliefs and practices. I see relevant elements and practices in Christianity, Hinduism, Buddhism, and the amalgam of New Thought. Some might say that means that I have no conviction or practice. However, I feel I've got conviction around the things that I believe, and I practice regularly to establish a personal relationship with God. From that standpoint I'm okay. I have beliefs and practices that bring me closer in my connection to the infinite. What is significant is not the label but the connection and direct personal experience.

The act of practice and devotion is the key. I was privileged to be able to hear one of the great American Buddhist masters, Lama Surya Das, speak and answer questions for an evening, and he made a comment that was extremely telling. In a discussion about the ways to Nirvana (or God), the Infinite, he noted that when we start to become overly rigid in our practice—whatever that might be—we start to run into more obstacles to our true connection, and we end up believing our path is the *only* path. He then went on to say that the path then becomes just another of the many *only* ways to God. How true. When I think back to my youth, much of the teaching about God was focused on the prescription for getting to heaven, and the *only* way to get there was by following the doctrines of a particular church.

As you see more of the world around you, you see a number of other paths. As each path begins its dogmatic narrowing to the *only* way to find God, our search turns from a personal connection to the divine into a rigid prescription for how to practice. It becomes exclusive of open, creative, and God-given thought, and turns into a rote practice of going to church at certain times, praying and meditating in certain ways and times, and following whatever doctrine the *only* way to God describes. While those practices and processes are not inherently poor choices, the typical progression is that those practices are monitored and managed (or at least clearly laid out specific requirements to get to heaven) by the church.

At this point organized religion can become less of a spiritual experience and more of a workaday process where we "punch the clock" of religion and then go back to our regular lives. Thus, we expect the church to take care of our spirituality, much as an employer takes care of our pay and insurance—as long as we punch the clock. How many of us go through the motions of church just like we do work (and unfortunately, many times, our lives in general)? While we might enjoy our work and do a good job, we know we have a "life" outside of work, and we go back to that at the end of the day and on the weekends and on vacation, and so on, forgetting (as best we can) the tasks back at work.

Religion can be the same way: We go to church but know that once it is over, we'll go back to our "life" outside of church and forget about the tasks of church work. We sit in the pew on Sunday playing our role as parishioner and thinking how good it feels and wishing there was some way to keep that feeling throughout the week. Then by Tuesday (if we're lucky; Sunday night if not), the warm glow of Sunday's spiritual encounter is lost in the fray of looming deadlines, family arguments, bills to pay, and taking the cat to the vet.

The main difference between church and work is that church—read: any religious practice—is usually limited to at best a few hours a week, maybe a couple on Sunday then another during the week. And so, when our religious prescription and process becomes the center point of our spiritual world, we've abdicated our spiritual responsibility. We've taken the responsibility for building and maintaining a spiritual relationship with God out of our hands and put it into the hands of the church. Organized religion is more than happy to do that, as this is what maintains their power and presence. For us, however, it is not very effective when it comes to truly establishing a personal relationship with God and allowing us to live our lives in God Confidence.

Parmahansa Yogananda said that the goal of all religions is (or should be) for individuals to establish a personal relationship with God. But how can we do that when we simply go through the motions a few hours a week? Now most churches will provide goals for living in God-communion throughout the week and tout that we must live the message all the time. However, if we just count on our few hours a week in the pew as our church work, how can we expect to build any sort of real, lasting, and habitual (meaning the things we do and the way we live is our nature) relationship with the Infinite?

While structured religion is a key part to any practice, it is not the only part and not a required element. We'll talk later about daily practices to help us establish habits and about the framework for a relationship with God. But let's contemplate on Lama Surya Das's words that there are many *only* paths. So let's take *any* of the *many*, because, if you take a cursory look at most major religions, they all share common themes. And I would find it hard to think that multiple, truly distinct Gods would come up with the same themes for each of their religions. Moreover, whether there is one or many, if you look at these basic tenets, they all lead to the same end. So if, like me, you believe that there is only one power and presence in the universe, and we are all from and part of it, then there are many ways to access it. Or, if you choose to consider only one path as the true way to God, the end result is the same. In each religion, regardless of the name, if you think, believe, and live in the right way, you will get to heaven. You will find "heaven on earth," so to speak. Again, the names are different but the end game for them all is the same: heaven, eternal bliss, nirvana, and so on.

So take one path or many, but believe and live God Confident, and we will all see the same reward.

However, what organized religion has done in some circles is to focus on requirements for how to live our lives (which in most instances is not necessarily bad as there can be some good that comes from that, except in instances of extremism). Religions want to define what our afterlife (you know it's not really an after-life, it's just life, because life never ends—so maybe *afterbody* or *nextlife* is a better term) will be like, either good or bad, so as to enter into a competition for souls. They attempt to make their way just a little different and with some unique tenet that will tip the scales in their favor and draw greater followership. But competition is a worldly thing rather than a spiritual one and thus religions have tried to distinguish themselves for the purpose of tipping those scales. Granted, many of the differences between religions are cultural and historical, but a number are manmade, nearly arbitrary, and in no way tied to God.

Despite the competition for followers and the attempts to distinguish themselves from one another, I'd like to focus on the similarity of religions rather than the differences. I think we'll see these similarities really demonstrate that no matter the "religious identity," there is a commonality at the base of them all. There is a singular point, a source that can be tapped into regardless of the religion. All religions strive to find and commune with God (whatever the name or format may be), and thus the religion itself becomes unimportant in relation to the ultimate goal and one's personal relationship with God.

So what do nearly all "great religions" have in common?

Belief in a Higher Power

The idea that there is a power and presence that is greater than our human form is a consistent message in all religions. While the type varies from a divine being to a cosmic consciousness to an ultimate awareness, we find this theme that there is something more to our lives. This belief could be argued to be born of fear, or a desire to somehow make ourselves greater than we are by pointing to something beyond to hold on to and to provide comfort and explanation to the pain and unexplainable. However, it could also be so consistent in description (and some would say scientific proof) that it is real, and our lives and those of billions of others are a part of something greater.

The major religions of the world all hold some form of deity worship, a higher power in the form of a divine being. From the Christian belief in God to Islam's Allah and Hindu's Brahman, each holds a higher being as God. Furthermore, each constructs their system around that deity and establishes practices to pay respect to the deity and, subsequently, establishes spiritual rules for living in the way of their particular religion.

What is notable in all these is that the behaviors of all these deities are really similar, and the role they play in the religious ceremony is the same. In general these beings are spirit, all knowing, all powerful, everywhere present, and the final authority (for lack of a better word). So to me it would seem there is actually a single power with different names.

When we look at our "communication" with God, we find that through prayer and meditation we tap into that higher power, and the experiences that come during prayer and meditation are real. Again, the sheer number of "experiences" that have been described over the millennia, and their commonality, lead to a conclusion that there is a higher power and that power is experienced through prayer, meditation, and contemplation.

And while I'm not really trying to convince you that there is a God, I am demonstrating that regardless of the religious path, the concept of a higher power is consistent across the religious spectrum. In addition, the teachings and experiences around this concept are so similar that coincidence and randomness are untenable explanations.

Afterlife

The age-old question: What happens when we die? Father Guido Sarducci (a comic character in the seventies and eighties) had an interesting take, saying that when we die our soul leaves the body in the form of a floating bubble and that bubble would float to heaven. How high our soul floated, and how close we got to heaven, depended on how good we were in life: the better we were the higher we floated. The saintly would make it to heaven straightaway, but the sinners might float just above the grill at the local greasy spoon diner (hell?). Those in-between would spend time at various levels between the deep fryers at the Twilight Grill and heaven—a sort of purgatory—until they'd paid for their sins and could float a bit higher and higher until they make it all the way to heaven.

I'm not sure Father Sarducci had the process completely correct. (To be honest, Father Sarducci wasn't really a Father. Although the liner notes to the comedy cassette [kids, ask your parents what a cassette is, or just Google it, as I realize some parents may be in the CD/digital-only generation] said he was a real Catholic priest, I've got my doubts). In any event, and humor aside, the afterlife is a significant tradition in the Christian religion. The concept of heaven or nirvana is a part of the other major religions too.

While some religions emphasize the soul's ascension to heaven as the focus of the afterlife, other traditions move in the way of reincarnation. The idea espoused is that following death, we come back to this human form again in another life and continue this process until we've worked out all our earthly issues (read: Karma) and have rediscovered our divine nature and spiritual bliss. And much like Father Sarducci's bubble soul floating at the level that matches our good in life, the next life in human form for the reincarnated will be based off where we were spiritually in the former life, the idea being that in each successive life we move closer and closer to the ideal until finally we escape the bonds of this earthly mortal existence and become one with the infinite.

While the theology and nuance of each religion's afterlife concepts could be discussed forever, the simple similarity of something beyond this human form, and an unfolding of a process to get to an ultimate point, cannot be discounted, and surely points to a singular source or destination regardless of the actual route taken.

Faith in the Divine/Unknown

The idea of faith is a significant point in religious practice. Whether the faith is a specific tenet about God, in the power of prayer, or contemplation and meditation, faith is a substantial component of nearly all religious practices. The idea is simple: There are things unknown and unexplainable that we, as practitioners of a particular religion, must believe regardless of the amount of proof that may be available. We accept that it is true based on faith. Whether that faith is that there is a God and a heaven and I'll get there by diligent practice, or that I'll be cured from a disease without medical intervention, or that I can find God through meditation, religions have a "requirement" around believing things that can't be proven. The idea of faith is so pervasive that it extends beyond the religious realm to our everyday lives. There is the faith in one another to do things that have been promised, faith that The System works, and faith that all will get their due at some point.

So why not extend that to faith in the process of life, and put our faith in the belief that the universe is always looking out for us and our good? Why not extend that faith to living our lives in a manner that is consistent with faith in us, and our connection with God ... extend it to God Confidence?

Forms of Practice and Ritual

Ritual is usually a significant part of any religious service and is really the overarching precept for the religion itself. There is in all practice an element of solemnness that affords a higher level of respect for the practice in a religious setting. As with many things, the specificity of a particular thing can cloud the landscape and actually hinder and disconnect one from the objective. So when our worship becomes about the practice of going to church, or a confession, or a prayer because *it is time to pray*, it can become a burden that is done not out of zeal and devotion but out of obligation. On the other hand, ritual with respect, solemnness, and goal-oriented focus on finding God is a crucial part of all religious regimens. And because of the consistent theme of practice and ritual, we have another factor in the argument that the specifics of the practice don't matter. What does matter are the practices with the goal of better establishing your relationship with God, and this is the key that crosses religious boundaries.

The key to any practice is knowing and being focused on the goal. Later we'll go over a number of practices that can be used, along with standard and common religious practices, to help hone the skills of better knowing ourselves and establishing a relationship with the infinite. Not only must we know what to practice, but *how* and with what *end* in mind, and only we can define that for ourselves. That's how it gets meaning and traction for us. If it's prescribed by someone else, no matter how true it may be, the significance is much less than if we give it meaning through personal desire.

Group Attendance

In most major religions there is some sort of regular attendance in a house of worship. Whether that is a church, temple, or synagogue, the concept is the same: the gathering together of likeminded souls in a ritual in a sacred space. Those services are the link for the common man to the holy and to God, the organization of the religion and the institutionalization of the practice for the masses. This is meant to be a truly joyous and uplifting experience, where the energy of a large group of people focused on a singular experience is, well, *spiritual*. It gives you kinship in the spiritual journey and motivation to continue to be a part of the community. The energy generated by the group of individuals working together is greater than the sum of them worshiping separately, and therefore helps all involved in their spiritual progress.

But, let's not allow it to become just something we do at that given hour. We must give ourselves over fully to the focus of the experience, not thinking about what's for lunch, or work the next day, or the goofy tie the guy in the fourth row is sporting, but focus on the moment, on God. We must give the group practice a single, pointed concentration that befits our goals and purpose, which is knowing ourselves and God, and establishing a personal relationship with God.

Communication with a Higher Power

As with group attendance, individual (and group) communication with the divine is a key aspect of religious practice. The concept here is that you must establish a connection and communicate directly with God, or communicate through some other holy being to send your thoughts to God. This communication takes many forms/ names but is really all a variation of a theme.

Probably all people are familiar with prayer, or talking to God in the language of your heart, as Parmahansa Yogananda puts it. Prayer is stillness and quiet allowing the practitioner to communicate with God through calling God's name and praising God. This can also be done through prayers of gratitude, forgiveness, grace, and support, or requests for general or specific outcomes. In any event, prayer is the opportunity for us to talk to God.

On the other hand, we have meditation. While it's been said that prayer is talking with God, meditation can be thought of as listening to God. I think the keystone of meditation is giving yourself time to be with spirit and without distractions. In *A Course in Miracles*, from the Foundation of Inner Peace, on page 486, it states, "the memory of God comes to the quiet mind." Meditation is time to be with yourself and God in the still silence, without judgment or movement, to just sit and feel and breathe. It is a time of quieting the mind to the outside "noise" of the world as well as to internal chatter, and giving ourselves time to be in the presence of God. Meditation is a calm stillness that allows us to be at peace and at one with God. Maybe it is listening, or maybe it is just being quiet enough to hear. Regardless, meditation is a key practice in a number of religions (especially from the East) and has numerous benefits both spiritually and physically, such as stress reduction, lowering of blood pressure, mental clarity and focus, among others.

There are other types of activity that can be a part of a religious practice, but they are all gathered into the categories of group attendance and communication. At its heart, religious ritual is about the connecting of the individual with the infinite by building a bridge to God though individual and group practices.

Basic Guidelines for Living: The Golden Rule

Most (if not all) religions prescribe some measure of "how to live." It can be encapsulated in the theme of the Golden Rule: Do unto others as you would have them do unto you, or variations on that theme, such as do no harm, do better, and so on. Or, the concept may be laid out in a great deal of specificity with instruction for a daily agenda and guidelines for every aspect of one's life. Regardless of the detail, across the spectrum, the message is similar: One should live a certain way in order to have the best chance of a holy afterlife, and to spread the acceptance of religious behaviors as much as possible.

This is certainly a noble perspective. But how often do we simply treat others well as a regular course of action in our daily live versus treating others well to get something in return? Are we living the Golden Rule because it feels good or because we fear the repercussions a particular religion says will befall us if we don't? While the Golden Rule is a broad spiritual concept, it has been co-opted by religions as a fear-oriented tool for compliance: "Do right by others or you'll burn in hell." And thus, the concept of right living is practiced based on a fear of consequence rather than a joy of living. It is focused on an end result rather than on a spiritual connection that makes the journey better for all. Let's take this opportunity to view it from the standpoint of doing right for God, and for the benefit of all beings in their divine glory. We can choose to follow the Golden Rule because it's the right thing to do, not because we'll get brownie points with "the man upstairs."

These consistent spiritual themes have been echoed across the millennia, in the world's cultures and religions from advanced to basic. Divinity, afterlife, faith, ritual, prayer, and right living have been codified in writings spanning thousands of years, and via a multitude of religions. So if the themes are the same and the teachings are in common, it would seem to indicate that there is something bigger out there, and it is constant and the same for all. And today science is beginning to prove this through the study of quantum physics. Our opportunity then is to live our lives with the confidence that we are a part of the infinite, and to realize that God is in us and with us every day, in every way. Thus we are, whether we choose to express it all the time or not, God Confident.

3

Sports as Divine

There is no glory in practice, but without practice, there is no glory.

—Unknown

(A quick side note before starting this chapter: If you have disdain or feel apathy toward sports, please read this chapter anyway, and just substitute music, dance, painting, quilting, or whatever activity you can relate to for the term sports, and you'll be just fine. Just as we have discussed that "God" can have many synonyms, so too can "sports.")

SOME MIGHT DOUBT the idea that sports and God are related, and be even more doubtful that sports can be a guide and example of spirituality in our modern world. But for all of you that worship your team and find Sunday a day for football more than a day for church, I say, this chapter is for you. For those of you who disdain sports as a boorish waste of time, this chapter is for you too. Because despite all the love for, hate of, or basic indifference to sports, sports is one of the most apt metaphors there is for life.

In sports and in life, you win some and you lose some, and you will experience some really high highs and some really low lows. In sports and in life, you can find a place to experience your passion and talent at various levels: in sports, from professional competition to weekend warrior to mere spectating, and in life, from career professional to hobbyist to a simple interest in a particular topic. And in sports as in life, if there is something we're interested in, connected to, and engaged in with a vested interest, we continue our involvement in the activity. Our engagement and involvement is out of love. How else can we explain Kansas City Royals fans (insert your lovable loser team of choice here), or the endless hobbyists, weekend warriors, and hacks of all sorts with limited talent continuing to sing, dance, paint, or play an instrument? It is the pure joy in what they are doing, enjoyment that comes from within. And most importantly, it is an individual confidence in them and in the activity, and the inner joy and peace it brings. *And, in sports as in life, you truly do get out what you put in.*

My sports experience is centered on running. My running career spans from my start with a halfhearted season of cross-country as a freshman in high school to my current quest to run a marathon in all fifty states. In all that time the one truth has been that I get out what I put in. When I slacked off on those high school runs through the park, it showed in not being able to make the freshman team. (I think I recall being able to run in a couple of meets but never being counted as a point-garnering runner.) On the other hand, when I put in good miles combined with sessions on the track and some core work, I've been able to complete marathons and improve on my times.

Likewise, in life, when I've really dedicated the time and committed to something, I've seen great results. However, when I've just idled along, I've gotten exactly that level of reward back. So the moral is *do* more, *get* more, and subsequently *be* more.

If we explore the nuances of any performance activity, particularly sports, we find many, many parallels with our individual and social lives. For instance, the ebb and flow of a game or event is much like the ebb and flow of our lives, and even each day within our lives. Much like the anticipation for the start of a game, there is the excitement of the start to a new day and what will it hold. There is the anticipation of getting to do the things we've planned and prepared for, and some apprehension around whether or not we are truly ready.

Additionally, there is the overarching tone of getting to be involved and participating in our day (or at least there should be). Then there is the drudgery of the daily grind, such as meetings, conversations, and basic events where our day goes up and down, high and low. Just like a game, or a good play followed by a penalty, followed by a lull in energy where the game just drags on. Our connection to spirit is no different: It ebbs and flows as well, with moments of excitement followed by disconnectedness, or the connection being pushed to the background by the drone of the noise of our daily lives.

They key is to have a focal point, a clear goal that you continually keep your eye on and can practice toward, becoming better and closer to reaching your goal. The other critical factor is to be able to be consistent through it all, much like coaches tell players to stay mentally in the game at all times and ride out the good and bad while focusing on winning. We too must us tell ourselves to stay connected, enjoy the excitement, and use that to fuel us through the difficulty. Even though the boss may be yelling, or a ton of extra stuff gets dumped on us at the last minute, we can remain in the game and focus on doing the best job we can, completing each task given with grace and proficiency.

Just as the team or individual knows, regardless of whether you win or lose, there will be another game. We too know that whether the day ends with sunshine or clouds, there will most likely be another.

And how we *played* is what is really important. One of the knowings of God Confidence is knowing that everyone is doing their best at any particular moment. That is our challenge too: working and striving to do our best in any particular moment regardless of the perceived struggle or drudgery of the specific task.

Let's look at the various levels of spirit in sports, and the basic concepts each may have to offer us as a parallel or example for our own spiritual practice and quest for a personal relationship with God. First, for those that participate, they are usually touched with God-given talents. No one can dispute that those that play sports at a professional level are gifted, both physically with size, speed, and strength, and mentally with intelligence, drive, and desire. While many are blessed with these characteristics, those in professional sports have them in spades. And they recognize that God-given talent. How many times do we see athletes give thanks and acknowledgment to God? Some might perceive this as disingenuous or self-promoting, but we can also view it as a true acknowledgment of gratitude. And, at the very least it can be a reminder to us that there is a connection in all aspects of life between humans and God.

Can we say those in sports are more divinely blessed than those of us in other walks of life? Perhaps, as I don't recall anyone ever walking out of a business meeting and pointing skyward, but maybe it has happened. While we may not point skyward, I'd guess it happens more frequently, in many walks of life, in a very quiet, personal, and nonobvious way. Or at least we have the chance to consider doing that. It could also be that the athlete knows there is a fine line in all sports between optimal performance and a career-ending injury, between making the play and playing the goat, so the closeness to the divine may be stronger due to the tenuous nature of the gift and the game.

While levels of competition vary, most everyone from the weekend warrior to the noncompetitive among us has been blessed with certain talents, physical skills, and mental capacities to move in our bodies. So you don't have to be a pro to reap the benefits of the divinity of sports. Any form of participation in sports or any performance activity is an exercise of divinity. Using the body, skill, and intelligence required to participate in anything at any level is an acknowledgment of the God-given life force within each of us, and an expression of the divinity inherent in us.

The very practice of competition and training forces one to be in the moment, to experience the connection of thought and action, and that space is where God is. When I run, I am grateful that I can, that some force is moving me forward and giving me the inner strength to keep going. I know that some runs feel really good while others are a struggle, but I know that there is a force beyond me that is involved in the process. I tap into a river of divine blessing flowing through me to help move me down the road, and can call upon this power when "hitting the wall." Some people call this being in the flow or "runner's high," but I call it God Confidence.

From the aspect of watching sports, the events and play shed light onto the spiritual nature of sports. How many times have we heard a sports announcer say "the atmosphere in here is electric" or "you can feel the intensity and energy in the stadium"?

That is God.

That feeling is thousands of people with energy focused on a single thing. That focus and feeling extends beyond each individual to the whole. People are "caught in the moment," "swept up in a sea of emotion," or otherwise experiencing something that is coming from within and something that is outside of them—and is bigger than them. That is a feeling to remember and anchor, because that is the feeling of living with God Confidence.

A personal experience with God comes from within and is bigger than oneself. We experience the same feeling of joy, excitement, and bliss. While there may be different causes, the feeling is what is similar and can act as a guide. Being able to experience a feeling and know that it can come from multiple sources allows us to use that feeling as a guide to help us know when we're doing things right and when we need to make adjustments to attain that feeling. Understanding that we can experience the feeling of electricity and joy in our daily lives in a way similar to the energy and excitement of a sporting event is an important reminder of the power of God Confidence, and ultimately our own power.

The key to the energy and excitement of sporting events is being caught in the moment. Being totally engaged in the event, not thinking about dishes to wash, or what's for dinner, or what we should have said at the meeting yesterday, it is about *experiencing* and *feeling* an event. It is about allowing ourselves to truly feel all of a happening and be a part of it. It is what makes live events so special, the atmosphere, as it is known, but really it is the individual simply being fully in the particular moment.

I know too many times I've kept myself from truly enjoying an event (sporting or otherwise) because I was engaged elsewhere, thinking about other things, caught in regret or fear, or feeling self-conscious about how my action might be viewed by others. And what did I leave that event with? A memory of something that was cool, but not quite what it could have been, and an experience that trained me how to react—in a way I really didn't want. It should be noted that noticing our feelings and reflecting on them is so critical to improving. If we just experience and never evaluate afterward how it felt or where our mind was, we may train ourselves to participate at a level that is less than complete. But by noticing a disconnection with the events, we can make improvements, which will improve our experience and make our practice better next time.

Again, much like running, we can practice all we want, but if we're practicing the wrong way we never really improve. In fact, we may even limit our performance. If I just go out and run slow, I'll get some benefit, but if my objective is to run fast, I have to practice some fast running to know what that feels like and to establish a confidence that my body is capable of running fast. Enjoyment of our life's events is the same thing. We have to practice really letting ourselves be engaged in the moment. If we don't, we condition ourselves (if we don't practice) to a feeling that is less than what it could be. So allow yourself to get caught up in an event, in the moment, and be invested, and then reflect on how that makes you feel.

From the perspective of a participant, have you ever been *in the zone*? A number of the greats from various sports have talked about being *in the zone*. The term has become synonymous with incredible performance. Where or what is *the zone*? My thought is that it is an extended connection with God. It is being completely present in the moment and in the flow of life.

From some elite athletes it has been described as if the game and all the other players are going in slow motion while the player in the zone is going at full speed. It manifests as periods of intense focus where they see things almost before they happen and put themselves where they need to be. There is a feeling that they are a step ahead, stronger and relaxed, seeing and feeling as if they are not playing the game but *are* the game, singularly linked to the moment. When asked about what helped him be a great player, hockey great Wayne Gretzky said that "I go to where the puck is going to be, not where it is."

This zone is not the exclusive domain of athletes, as performers in other realms enjoy this same experience of extreme focus when every note comes easily; the steps of the dance are light and precise with every movement being effortless and flowing; jumps are higher; spins are faster; the voice is clearer and stronger. It is all in an effortless oneness with themselves and the activity—no thought, just action. It is all intense focus while sharing a God-given gift, in the sincere joy of doing something that is loved.

So let us transfer being in the zone from performance events to our daily lives. What a great example of how to live each day. We can live and act with extreme focus and concentration, doing something we love in joy, while noticing everything around us is seemingly moving in slow motion. We can realize that we come up with exactly the right word or action in the moment it is needed. We can act with supreme confidence in our ability with a singular objective to live this day as no other, in confidence and joy, and as a benefit to all beings around us.

Another key component of sports as a metaphor for the divine and our daily lives is the reality of the impermanence of the ups and downs, the highs and lows of the process of preparation and competition. It is often said that one of the most important characteristics of a successful athlete is a short memory. A player cannot be too caught up in their recent success or failure, because the next play can change all of that. If a player commits a mistake on one play, they must immediately move on to the next play and focus on their responsibility and performance in that moment. The same is true for a concert pianist or ballet dancer; the performance continues to move, and they cannot be concerned with a mistake. They must instead move past it and work toward completion of a body of work that will be perceived as wonderful regardless of the mistake.

Likewise, a performer can't be too caught up in a great performance because it is a continually moving process. Any lack of focus, or attention on their past glory, can cause a lapse later on. Sports may be one of the most "what have you done for me lately" ventures we have. One day you're a hero while the next day you are being run out of town. So to be successful you must focus on the now. Clearly we can learn from mistakes and enjoy success, but it must be done—as with so many things—in moderation and at the appropriate time.

So too in life we must accept the impermanence of circumstances and life itself. We can't be overly concerned by things we deem as mistakes, nor celebrate too long on our victories. The adage of staring so longingly at the door that just closed that we miss another opening is so apt, and sports and daily life are such clear examples of this idea. The greats of the game are passionate, but usually very level headed. They don't beat themselves up over mistakes, but quickly assess how they will perform differently next time. They don't linger over their successes, but anchor the feeling of success to lay the foundation of future greatness.

The acceptance of impermanence also plays a key role in our formulation of a personal relationship with God. We grow to understand that things are constantly changing, and that those external circumstances, because of their inherent impermanence, cannot be what defines us. The Buddhist religion actually teaches that suffering comes from our attachment to impermanent things. As we relate more closely with God, we come to find joy in ourselves and in God, and not in the circumstance. Moreover, much like the great athlete measures success based on a career, a body of work over time that demonstrates consistency and goodness, we too must measure our relationship with God and the living of our lives on the totality of our actions and intention on the body of work we develop and the consistency with which we live.

We need to avoid getting caught up in moments of fear, lack, and unskillful practice, or in moments of compassion and generosity, but rather in the overarching compilation of our life. In general are we striving to build a better personal relationship with God and thereby those around us? If so, celebrate that, and anchor that feeling to continue to build consistency in our practice and expansion of ourselves and our good and God. If not, celebrate that we have the awareness to recognize and reflect on what needs improvement, and the opportunity to get better. Much like the player who's not performing as he or she'd like to, the ability to assess their performance and commit to practice and improvement can be the fresh start, and the change that revives a career—or a life.

We come to rejoice over success and mourn failure, but only for a moment because it was an event that happened in our lives, but did not happen to us. What happened to us was our reaction to the event, and that is controlled by us and continually elevated by our personal relationship with God. Sports exemplify this process. Players/coaches/owners routinely serve as the great savior one day and the bum that should be run out of town the next. But in reality they are neither, they are all children of God—people using their God-given talents in an expression of joy. Let us live in the same manner, knowing that the champion and the also-ran are the same. The stronger our relationship with God, the greater our confidence that we are not our successes or failures, but a compilation of how we behave in light of those circumstances. In God Confidence we can live life fully and from the inside out. Not lingering in celebration or woe, but learning how to experience our world from moment to moment.

Confidence is another key element in sports that has a great correlation to our daily lives. Athletes are often judged as cocky, arrogant, and very full of themselves. And while it may be accurate that in some instances when that personality trait is a bit over the top, some measure of confidence is required to play successfully. Likewise, some measure of confidence is necessary for each of us to live wholly (holy).

In an interview on sports talk radio, college basketball coach Frank Martin was asked about whether a particular player was gaining confidence and playing better. Martin responding by saying yes, and noted that confidence is made up of the individual feeling good about him- or herself and putting the work in during practice in order to see results. This is exactly the same process as when we talk of our God Confidence. We must feel good about ourselves and put in the work in daily practice to the point that we start to see results. One without the other is a starting point but not the level of confidence that allows one to step into any daily situation and enjoy that situation and know it is exactly right. Without confidence we are tentative and tend to over-think situations. That thinking then takes us out of the flow and connection with the event. Without effective practice, which demonstrates results, we don't think/know what we are capable of. And until we think/know we can do a thing, success is a challenge.

Thus, practice is such a vital element in sports and in life. It helps us rehearse the right way to do things and builds skills, execution, and the *confidence* that a certain thing can be done. That in turn makes the player feel better about their ability to execute and, when game time comes, they are better equipped to perform. Then performance in the game builds an even greater confidence that spills back to practice: I practiced it; the game went well, so if I practice more, it gets even better. This approach applies to all performance-based events. In my running, I know I have to prepare to run. When I first started running I ran slow and not very far, but as I ran over and over again, those slow, short distances became easier. I then had the confidence to start running farther and faster. As I run more I see that the practice has paid off in the short, slow runs becoming faster and longer, and so I do more and the process builds on itself.

If we think of this process in terms of building a personal relationship with God, the same is true. We start with short, simple prayers or meditations, and we begin to notice a feeling of comfort and happiness. We then notice that feeling expanding to our daily lives, and we devote more time and energy to the prayer and meditation, and notice even greater happiness and comfort, and finally, confidence. Taking this process further and making it a habit is a challenge.

Because, just like the athlete that makes a mistake or chokes in a pressure situation despite the practices, we may have setbacks or not see results as quickly as we'd like. And, just like the athlete, we must continue to trust in the process, refine how we practice and know our job is the practice. We must also be aware of how that practice makes us feel and thus tweak and refine it so that we continue to improve.

Part of that improving practice involves a great deal of spirituality. While it may not be called that in the sports world (more common vernacular would be sports psychology), it is the same thing. Part of the success or failure of team sports is often attributed to chemistry. What is that? At its most basic level, chemistry is teammates trusting one another, and having a feel for each other as well as their strengths and weaknesses. It is playing together and having an energy and confidence that as a team they can do anything. It is energy. For a scientific term like chemistry, that description sounds anything but scientific. There is no way to measure trust, teamwork, or confidence. But when we think of what chemistry stands for, the ability—lo I say, the *practice*—of combining various elements to create another distinct element, it starts to make a bit more sense. And if we think in terms of spirituality, it really comes together.

When we think of spirituality, we're looking at the practices of taking things, somewhat undefined or at least not scientifically testable (although that is starting to change), and making them into a product. The goal is a life that shows definable and definitive results. We take things like meditation, prayer, intention, and visualization and turn them into daily performances. We practice life, where we interact and, ideally, are a beneficial presence for ourselves, to others, and to our world. We are a part of the infinite flow of life, connected to something larger and really enjoying our lives (as Eckhart Tolle says, enjoy = in joy in ourselves).

So we have and experience chemistry in our lives. We trust in the process of life, how it will react to us (and us to it), and "the flow of the game." Ultimately, we can create a chemistry between ourselves and the infinite by getting to know the team (ourselves, God, and the process of life), practicing (see chapter 5: "Practice Is the Key—Daily Ways"), and experiencing the successes of our life. When we create this chemistry and it becomes something greater than ourselves, we and God are a team that can be champions in this game we call life.

Another component of sports psychology is the idea of visualization. The notion here is that we see in our mind what success looks like before participating in the event or activity. We formulate in our mind a vision of our best performance, and we replay that scene over and over to condition our minds and emotions to the feeling that comes from that vision. When we see a positive outcome, we prepare the mind and body for what that looks like and how it feels, with the idea that it will be more likely to come about in reality if we've thought about it and visualized it previously.

Many teachers, from business to sports to life, talk of beginning with the end in mind. For our sports analogy, we hear the cheering crowd, see the final score on the scoreboard, and feel the success and sense of accomplishment. Then we work backward to our individual performance and the process of the game.

From a runner's perspective, we visualize a great run. We see ourselves crossing the finish line strong as we look up to the clock and see our goal time. We feel the exhilaration of having done our best and beating our goal. We relish in the tired but rewarding feeling of hitting the mark and the joy of all the work paying off. We then replay the race and feel ourselves feeling strong and relaxed over the final few miles, knowing that we've hit the splits necessary to our PR (personal record; most runners keep track of their best times in various distances and will strive to better those times, trying to a PR at a race). We see ourselves feeling comfortable through the middle part of the race, running relaxed and free and knowing that came from the strong, controlled start and a powerful run through the early miles.

We do this mental practice time and time again, then we do it before our long training runs and then finally in the race, the idea being that we can trick our mind into believing we can do something we've not yet done and to condition ourselves to the feelings of winning, victory, and success. By seeing it happen and feeling *that* success, we make welcome the victory we imagine and our bodies and minds begin to understand what success is like. We practice to condition our bodies, and likewise we should practice to condition our mind and emotions.

My youngest daughter implemented this notion of visualization to perfection at a horse show one time. She was competing in a lead-line class, and as she and her mom were warming up for the event, she told her mom that she was going to win, and could see herself receiving the first-place trophy at the end of the class. They discussed holding on to that image throughout the warm-up and continued to focus on it during the class. My daughter's ride was flawless, and the result was just as she had envisioned—a first-place trophy. If all grade-school children could learn this concept, just think how wonderful their futures could be.

Our visualization and intention for life should be no different and should be practiced and executed on a daily basis to prepare us for our successes in work, family, social, and spiritual interests. We'll talk more about this in the daily ways chapter, but suffice it to say, it is practice and, moreover, work that establishes our routine and our tools for managing our lives and establishing God Confidence. It is also important to note that the training of body, mind, and emotions is just as important in the everyday realm as it is in the previous example of running and sports. In fact, it is that *feeling* that is really crucial to our success in training ourselves for our life.

The body and mind will sometimes allow themselves to be lulled into a false sense of security when it comes to life, and to spiritual life in particular. But our heart, the center of our feelings, will give us clues, and we must learn to be attentive and responsive to them. As with running, the body rewards you with better performance as you listen to it. You push when you're able and recover when the body demands, all in an effort to run longer and faster. From a spiritual perspective, we can apply this same concept to the heart. We are rewarded by our feelings becoming stronger and more reliable the more we are attentive to them. We then practice and thereby condition ourselves to respond when we notice a given feeling.

It will be easy to forget that any day or any hour is an opportunity to practice. It will be easy to discount when it works as nothing more than happenstance, and grouse when it doesn't as "that's just the way my life goes." However, it all comes down to confidence and reaping the rewards of doing the things necessary to establish confidence. It is also a bit of a risk, as building confidence means we're taking responsibility for our life, making a declaration that we can have some span of control over what happens to us. Again, it is much easier to write things off as "that's just the way it is" or "I got lucky on that one, but it won't happen again," than it is to diligently practice and say "I worked to make that happen" or "I came up short because I wasn't prepared."

For some reason we seem to attach a bit of a negative connotation to the word confidence, and assume that it is just a feeling or an attitude (and sometimes a bad one at that). When we talk about true confidence, God Confidence, we are talking about an experience. It is an experience that we feel and can recreate with practice.

True confidence in running is knowing that if I stick to a training plan in preparation for a race, I will have done everything I can to position myself to succeed. I have to take on the responsibility to execute the plan and then run the race. I have to be diligent in noticing how my body responds to the various workouts in the plan and subsequently how I respond during the race. I have to be willing to learn from that experience and adjust the plan for the next race. I have to continue that pattern of planning, practice, execution, awareness, adjustment, and more practice. It is an ongoing process that builds on itself, and I have to take the risk of trying it, running in the race, and then evaluating how I'm doing.

There are no guarantees that success will be immediate, but if I approach the activity, the practice itself, as something I enjoy, and understand that there will be benefits to what I'm doing beyond just the goal of a PR or the medal, I can be at peace and enjoy the practice. By not just focusing on the end result—no matter how sweet that may be—I can enjoy and accept the process, the time involved, and the living that I'm doing in the process. That's cool. It's cool because it opens up an entirely new perspective, a perspective where I have control over my actions, practice, and life. It is a perspective where I am risking something by assuming that control, but also where I am rewarded both in the action/process itself, as well as in the end result and the life I'm building. And that's the experience that leads to confidence. That is an experience that is noticed each day and practiced, and then noticed more and practiced more, expanded on, and made habitual. As we go along with the practice we are also reaping the benefits, small and large, and living that confidence, God Confidence. And as my wife and her college roommate used to say, "it is all practice for the big game." In sports and in life, it is the daily practice that matters most.

4

God Created Bad Drivers

Have you ever noticed that anybody driving slower than you is an idiot and anyone going faster than you is a maniac?

—George Carlin

I AM THE GREATEST driver in the world, or at least I used to be. Back in the day I would have other drivers on a near-weekly basis acknowledge my status as number one by giving me a single finger salute. I never once was concerned that they were using their middle finger instead of the usual raised pointer finger to indicate my lofty status. As a grumpy old man once told me, "Your honking horn is a sign of defeat." So too, I took the bird as a white flag of the highway.

Despite the chapter title, I don't really think God creates bad drivers. God allows us to perceive another driver as good or bad. You might ask why God would allow that sort of judgment. It is because one our greatest gifts is the freedom to choose in any moment how we will think, feel, act, and be. There is no divinely set rule for any given circumstance on how we must feel or experience it in any particular way, as it is up to each one of us to decide. One of the great human graces is our ability to choose how we feel at any given moment.

For me, that opportunity to pick a feeling and response provides me a chance to practice God Confidence. You see, the simple act of driving (or riding on the bus, or the subway, or biking, or walking) is a daily activity that puts us in the real, human world. And as such, it affords us the means to experience all the circumstances, happenstances, and emotions associated with moving about on planet earth.

But what God Confidence affords is not just living through the events or experiencing them in some sort of observer-only role. Rather it is a connection to the divine by way of the experience. It is in those experiences that we begin to learn to manage the process that supports not only an objective-observer self, but also a joyous-divine self. That divine self accepts, understands, and relishes the process of the experience and sees all experiences as divine. We begin, in God Confidence, to see the opportunity for connection with the infinite in every circumstance.

Driving, particularly in metropolitan areas, can be frustrating (if we choose to make it that way). With traffic jams, drivers going too fast or too slow, the hectic pace of the day, weather, road construction, and the like, there are any number of challenges keeping us from our destination. The days of the Sunday afternoon drive for relaxation are long gone—except for the one person right in front of me who's decided Monday morning at 7:45 a.m. is going to be their Sunday afternoon. In any event, compressed schedules and frayed nerves can make for a miserable commute. Even on the best days there seems to be a myriad of opportunities to be frustrated behind the wheel.

This frustration is really God's opportunity for us to practice. It is a chance for us to relinquish our perceptions and judgments of the events of the day and the ways of others. It is our chance to slip back into the presence, into ourselves, and make habitual the ability to face any circumstances with the aplomb of God Confidence. Yes, I'm saying that even the most frustrating of events and/or people are God's gift to us, a chance to practice our oneness with spirit. The more we practice, the better we get. Obviously, God knows we all need lots of practice, as there seems to be no shortage of frustrating and annoying circumstances in our daily lives.

The Three Rs

I think there are three steps one can choose to take when frustrated by the circumstances of the highway, or the office, or the house, or the day. These are the three Rs of daily life and one of the first practices we can implement to begin the process of establishing a life of God Confidence.

- **Realization**. We have the opportunity to practice noticing and awareness (third-party observer, our emotional guide).
- **Reflection**. We have the opportunity to practice nonjudgment (detachment and relinquish ego).
- **Replacement**. We have the opportunity to practice recalibration (where you want your vibe to be).

Realization: Noticing and Awareness

How often are we really thoughtful and aware of our actions and, more importantly, our feelings? I would venture to guess that most of the time most of us are not really aware of our feelings at any particular moment, and we go through life on autopilot. Oh sure, we get (and feel) angry or frustrated or happy. But how often do we consciously choose that feeling rather than it being a conditioned reaction to a circumstance? If you're like me, an unconscious reaction to an event is probably more frequent than a measured and chosen response. And, for a good many of us, that process goes unnoticed day in and day out. We don't take the opportunity to learn and grow from a very human condition of reacting to circumstances. Perhaps, more significantly, we probably don't know how to learn and grow from it, and may not know that we can.

Hence, the terms "habitual" and "reaction" both apply here. Both denote a very patterned and subconscious process that is a (at least in the common thought) "normal" practice of doing the same action in response to a similar circumstance. It has become accepted that the situation or the circumstance is the genesis of our behavior. However, the circumstance is merely the stuff that is happening around us. It is not happening to us or coming from us, but is simply going on around us. We get to choose how we will react to that stuff going on around us. And so, the first of the three Rs, realization, is the opportunity to notice, to realize that *we* control how we act, rather than the circumstances around us. We need to realize that what is most natural and beneficial is our controlling our emotions and actions, regardless of the circumstances. So while the "normal" response to being cut off in traffic might be to blast the horn and give the single-finger salute, the natural action is to ... we'll get to that in a bit, as we may know what we're doing is unskillful, but what to do differently or how we do something differently may not be clear yet.

In essence, we want to redefine our habitual reactions. We want to move from a seemingly uncontrolled behavioral response to a stressor to a thoughtful action that we choose and control. That action is expressed as being present, aware, and conscious, and confident in our actions so that they are our chosen prescriptions rather than habitual reactions.

This is a key to understanding, accepting, and practicing God Confidence. There are several layers at play here. "Understanding" is pretty obvious. It is the opportunity to see that there is a difference between habitual reaction and choosing how to act in each moment, and therefore controlling the moment. Now, no matter how difficult that might be to practice, understanding the concept of prescriptive selection versus reaction is probably a fairly easy leap.

Next, though, it becomes more challenging to accept the idea that we live in each moment. And to know that we are present, managing, controlling spirits that express God in each moment of our human existence is a tall order, and acting in that way is even taller. The challenge extends to knowing and accepting that we live in God Confidence or (more aptly) to remember our God Confidence as we accept and surrender to the opportunities that are provided each day.

When we accept that the moments of frustration in our daily lives are merely opportunities for us to practice our connection to spirit, and not the universe plotting against us, it is in that moment that we experience, no matter how fleeting, God Confidence. The moment we align our spiritual selves with our human selves is the moment we connect and live. We are truly alive in the moment and have the confidence that we are in control. That feeling is evidence (again no matter how fleeting) of our connection with God, and of our God Confidence.

This exercise and experience is tough because there is no one to blame at this point, no excuses, only us and our power/opportunity to choose. Once we accept God Confidence we can no longer be upset with the maniac changing lanes; the driver practicing the Art of Zen and Driving 30 mph in the Passing Lane; the rude person on the bus not offering their seat to a lady, and on and on. We have responsibility now for our own feelings and actions, and that is frightening. We must now accept we are the ones with the ill feeling somewhere inside, and we have to accept that we have lost our connection with God and the present moment. But, the reprise here is that this acceptance means we've acknowledged the opportunity and seen the situation not as a circumstance of our existence but as the nature of our existence. It is a situation that can be controlled, managed, and enhanced by the perspective we now have.

Acceptance and awareness is one part, but the practicing is a challenge too. Part of that challenge is that we initially go through the understanding and accepting each time we practice. We have the opportunity to practice daily, but to take advantage of those opportunities is often difficult. To do it we have to recognize in each circumstance that 1) we are disconnected, 2) we are actually in control, and 3) there is something icky going on inside us that's manifesting the discord we sense. Please note that the desire is for this condition to be temporary.

As we practice, the gap between recognition that we've become disconnected and reestablishing our connection becomes smaller and smaller until it is replaced altogether by our new habit of being present, aware, and God Confident. But in the interim, as we practice (from a running perspective, the interim is getting up to more weekly mileage or turning a faster lap on the track; neat goals, but getting there is sometimes a real bear, and there are no shortcuts), how do we stay positive and not beat ourselves up each time we have to live through this experience?

The answer is that it will require that each practice is a wind sprint of self-analysis, crunches of acknowledgment of our disconnections, and the burning pull-ups of *realization* that we could have done something differently if we hadn't been disconnected. But in each of those opportunities we know we are getting closer to more presence. Know that the mental blood, sweat, and tears are finally rewarded with the winning of being with spirit, in control of our actions and emotions, and living a God Confident life.

Reflection: Nonjudgment/Detachment

The next exercise is to be able to examine the circumstances that put you in a situation where your internal ill-ease has surfaced, seemingly out of nowhere due to the idiot in traffic, your jerk of a boss, or the barrage of demands on your time from family and friends. So we have to look at why you were running late, and, more significantly, why you were worried about it. We have to look at the *whys*. Were you late because you were having a deep conversation with your daughter about the type of caterpillar she'd just found in the garden? Or were you late because you spent a few more minutes in front of the TV catching up on the latest celebrity gossip?

The objective here is to perform some self-analysis, and allow yourself to notice your triggers of unconsciousness and disconnection, and then formulate thoughts that will establish new action patterns to ensure the situations that got you to this point are more closely managed in the future. It also allows us to see where and how our time is being spent.

The key is taking action. It doesn't mean subjecting yourself to mental flogging over the issue. It does mean practicing forgiveness—for yourself and others. It also means to look at things just as they are from a very detached and nonpersonal perspective. We often spend a good deal of time examining why a particular thing is good or bad, or what degree of goodness or badness it may have. Instead, if we approach the subject from a detached, nonjudgmental perspective, we can look at both the situation and the impact of our actions objectively. This reflection trains us to be more aware of how we feel in the moments before disconnection, and it allows us to identify the triggers of our habitual reactions. The idea is that reflecting on the cause of our disconnection and the feelings associated with it will allow us to see it coming sooner, and in essence break the cycle.

So if we know that traffic causes us problems we can leave a little earlier, or if not, then appreciate all the joy we experienced that caused us to be late. Moreover, we can then, hopefully, be prepared to deal with a potentially risky situation and go ahead and start the calming mantras and the acceptance that we are exactly where we need to be in this moment. Without reflection, it's just another chance to be upset and frustrated with the world around us, and ultimately with ourselves.

Replacement: Recalibration/Setting Presence

The idea of being able to control our emotions, thoughts and actions is extremely powerful. I would go so far as to say it is one of the great secrets of the ages. However, if we have nothing to think other than thoughts of woe, lament, fear, anger, and the like, we start to feel like we really don't have control, like we're just helplessly bobbing up and down in the ocean of life at the mercy of the tides. In large part the challenge for many folks is that they have allowed their circumstances to dictate the range of thoughts and emotions they allow themselves to experience. So much so that we even prepare ourselves for struggle (this meeting is going to be awful; I hate having to deal with so and so; it hurts to go to the dentist; or any number of preparatory statements and thoughts that have become habit.). We are fully prepared for a habitual response of difficultly in too many situations. The key is in knowing that our thoughts create our reality, and in order to change our reality we must recalibrate our thoughts.

Thus the idea of recalibration comes into play. Let's reset our level of expectation and feeling to a higher and more positive vibration. Let's prepare ourselves for ease and joy by coming up with replacement thoughts that feel good. Whenever a problematic situation arises, we first realize we are reacting, disconnected, and not present. We celebrate that realization as our opportunity to connect with God, and we reflect on what put us into the situation/feeling to begin with. We can then use that reflection to note the moment of struggle or disconnection and the emotion/feeling associated with it. Finally, we replace that negative emotion or thought with something more positive.

It can be anything really, a canned mantra or affirmation, something simple like "I am happy, healthy, and whole, and am perfectly where I need to be in this moment," or "the world is looking out for me, and this moment is what is needed for me to be safe and happy." Or it can be something more specific to the situation at hand. And, as is true with most things, the more specific or relevant it is to the situation, the better and more meaningful the replacement thought will be.

So if a project at work encounters a big problem, I may say "this is a chance to make the product better," or "this is an opportunity to learn and work with new people," or "I can give someone else a chance to shine," or maybe I say "this problem may have prevented some bigger problem later on."

Again, the key is that we are giving our minds and spirits options: more positive options in how to feel and what to think. This process also trains us to think in a more controlled manner. Even the process of thinking about replacement emotions or thoughts is one that gives us control of a circumstance, as it causes a break in the habitual pattern of our negative responses. So when I'm mad and thinking about all the trouble that is coming my way, the practice of replacement gives me an opportunity to break out of the "woe is me" cycle and think a different thought (demonstrate control over the emotions and take control back from the situation).

This process trains the mind to look for higher-level thoughts. They can be either personal affirmations or specific positives. And when practiced daily, they not only support changing our emotions and thoughts in that moment, but also train us to look for higher-level ideas in all situations.

So let's take an example of how to put this concept of the three Rs into practice. Say there is someone that you have to deal with on a regular basis that you find it difficult to get along with. It could be a coworker, family member, or someone else. It seems like every time you are around this person they are getting in your grill, criticizing you, or in some way trying to pick a fight. And every time they do this, you react with anger and irritation or feel that you have to defend yourself. You may even play the event over and over in your head for days afterward, thinking of all the things you wish you would have said.

By using the three Rs you can decide that you are going to change this relationship into a positive one. Note that it has to be *you* that changes, not the other person. First, you *realize* that this situation causes you to struggle, and it is your thoughts and negative feelings about this person that have caused you to feel bad. Then you *reflect* on why this is the case. Are you expecting them to be something they are not? Is it really you that is angry or causing part of the problem? Why does it matter anyway—is it really worth all the perceived pain and trouble?

Finally, you *replace* your thoughts, emotions, and subsequent actions toward the situation with a more positive script, one that you control. You might forgive them, either in your mind, in a letter, or even in person. You may even ask for their forgiveness for the way you have acted (this can be very powerful). Then you accept that they are doing the best they can, and they probably are hurting inside or are feeling badly about themselves.

It is *their* thoughts that are causing them to act in this way. You can change your thoughts to accept them as they are and to realize that it is not about you at all but about them. You can bless them in your mind and know that the divine is in them also, and that you are really connected on some level. You can agree with yourself that they will no longer create a problem for you, because you *have changed your mind* and your subsequent thoughts and emotions about the situation. You can imagine how good this will feel the next time you interact with them. Just give this a try, and you will find that the relationship will transform itself. Many spiritual teachers have taught that if you want to change others, you must first change yourself, and then they will benefit from that.

As with any pursuit, the more you practice, the better you will get. Like with running, the first few runs are tough, but as you do more it gets easier. The first few times you try to replace being pissed at the world or yourself with a rainbow- and puppy dog-infused dose of happiness, you may want to kick yourself, but it will feel better than the alternative. It will, if practiced, yield an easier experience next time and ultimately expand your mental vocabulary of positivism.

5

Daily Ways: Practice Is the Key to God Confidence

> *Practice means to perform, over and over again in the face of all obstacles, some act of vision, of faith, of desire. Practice is a means of inviting the perfection desired.*
>
> —Martha Graham

PART OF ANY endeavor is action: doing something with intent, direction, and a successful outcome in mind.

When running, one typically establishes some goal that one is striving for, such as running to improve health, running to complete a mile, a race, a marathon, or whatever. And, based on that goal, a training plan is established. When I decided I was going to get back to running, I outlined some high-level goals: complete a marathon in all fifty states and ultimately on all seven continents, qualify for the Boston Marathon, and run some specific times in the marathons. Based on these goals, I determined I was going to have to start running more (a lot more) and subsequently would have to really commit to a plan. So I leaned on the *Runner's World* training plan for marathons, and I started doing the runs described in the plan.

Additionally, I did something I'd never done before despite years of running. I started keeping a running log. This entails writing down the daily mileage, times, workouts, and cross training as I completed each workout. Folks who are experts in getting things done say you must write down goals, monitor progress, and evaluate successes and failures. I'm applying that to the running, and so far so good. It has meant sometimes running when I really didn't want to, getting up early (really early), and then being accountable to write down and track what I'm doing. Saying you plan to run forty or fifty miles a week is easy, thinking about it starts to make it seem possible, but actually doing it is another story. But doing it means I have been able to complete marathons.

This process has also shown me that when I have backed off the level of effort for training runs, or dropped a few miles, or not pushed my interval workouts, I've experienced struggles in my longer runs. On the other hand, when I have done my hard workouts, stuck to my plan, and pushed myself, I've seen better times and stronger finishes in my long runs. So practice and training for specific goals, having a plan and writing down the plan, and tracking the results works.

When we think about running or establishing new habits, such as becoming/living a God Confident life, we have to take action, practice, and train ourselves to be aware. We have to monitor and evaluate our progress and maybe even write things down. You could even do a meditation log. Write out a plan for your quiet times so they are scheduled just like you would any other important appointment. Then when completed, you can make notes about the meditations. Note how you felt and what you thought before, during, and after. This allows you to keep track of your focused quiet time and train your body and mind for the exercise and practice of meditation. In addition to a physical log, there are a number of smart phone apps that support meditation. One I'm using right now is called Self. It's a simple timer with some music and sounds, and it logs your meditations and allows you to make notes.

We can think about things all we want, and thinking is clearly the first step, as our thoughts create our reality. However, we have to act on the things we think about to promote change. We have to take action to manifest the thoughts we have. The minister at my church gave a great metaphor one time about this concept. It's like paddling a boat, with one paddle being your thoughts and the other being action. If you are just using one paddle (thought or action) without the other, you will just go around in circles.

While daydreaming may be enjoyable, it gets old, and at some point we determine that we must go beyond just being entertained by our thoughts and actually experience what's in them. Mary Morrissey discusses this idea of thought without action as just being entertainment in her wonderful program, *Prosperity Plus—A New Way of Living*. She discusses the significance of combining thoughts, intention, and visioning with action, accountability, and active participation in the manifestation of our lives. We have the choice to either build our dreams (action and accountability) or just go through the motions again and again (thinking about doing something, but not going beyond that).

With that in mind, we need to take actions that will support our growth, practice, and the manifestation of God Confidence in our lives. There are a number of things I'll summarize here that are easy, common, and supported by numerous authors, experts, and sages.

The great truth in all spiritual literature is that we don't need to *do* anything, but we should just *be*. However, in the early stages of our being many of us deal with struggles and frustration in our lives and with the whole concept of just being. When we're feeling stressed or depressed or angry, it seems a bit simplistic to say, "just be." In those moments it is very hard to understand how that works, or what it really means. The advice to just be happy, change your mind, and stay relaxed seems to be ignorant of *my* struggles and problems and lacks understanding. Moreover, that concept seems to show no compassion for the task of living life in the real world. So we need a process and tools to get us to the point of just being, tools to use daily so that we have something to *do* that ultimately allows us to *be*. Slowly but surely, these things we do become what we *are*.

We practice and make the habits that become our being so that the idea of just being becomes real. It just takes practice and patience, and for me, lots and lots of practice and patience. The daily ways (practice) are not really tools to get to a point; they *are* the point, both the destination and the journey. It only feels like we are doing something to get somewhere because of our current perception of the situation (read the section on nonsituational dependence). But, ultimately, the practice is the being: just be, and we begin to build a habit of being through the daily ways. We become content, and contentment is not bad. It just means we are being confident in the content and context of our lives.

To get started, take one or two of these daily ways, and establish your own practice of doing them every day, or even multiples times a day. As with running, when we want to establish a habit of going for a run, we sometimes have to start in very structured way. Specifically, we start by mapping out the time and distance of each run. Putting that regimen around the process initially "forces" us to go out and run, until we come to the point where going for the run feels normal. In essence, it becomes a habit, just like teeth brushing or eating breakfast, and we will feel odd if we don't get our run in.

The same is true with spiritual practice. We want to establish practices, and we plan and are very disciplined about doing them. Our goal is to make these elements habits in our life, to make them things that happen and we do as an action in our lives rather than a reaction to events. We want these things to support us in stressful situations where we have acted unskillfully (thoughtlessly, acting out of habit and not choice) and make them our new actions and choices. I prefer the term actions, but reaction is probably more descriptive here. Our desire is that we find these practices will, over time, reprogram our bad habits that form current reactions into new, improved God Confident habits and actions that support our spiritual way of life. This is a way of acceptance and accountability, a way of manifestation and joy, a way of trust and confidence that the events in our life are ours. And those events are ultimately good, regardless of the outward immediate appearance to the casual observer.

Establishing a sense of God Confidence and living from that is easier than you think—it just takes practice, lots and lots of practice. I truly think God Confidence is like running, or any other endeavor you hope to become proficient at: You practice and you'll see the rewards. You run and you see the rewards.

It is simple, but there are some key factors to keep in mind:

Be Diligent in Your Practice

We must be diligent in our practice, as the experience of success can be subtle, and you may miss it. The feeling of failure is obvious and powerful. We are quick to judge ourselves harshly if things don't go exactly as planned. But to elevate ourselves beyond our preconceived notions about our ability, we have to be willing to try. We have to assess those tries, not exclusively in the realm of wins and losses, but in terms of how we are moving on our arc of progression. We have to trust the plan and the process and not expect overnight success. If you don't trust the process and expect to see and feel significant changes immediately, you might miss the small progress you do make due to the subtle and gradual nature of the process. So we have to understand, respect, and trust the process, as this is really the first step in God Confidence.

Be Willing to Experiment/Evaluate

While there are some tried and true practices and plans for becoming a better runner, each runner is unique, and they have to experiment with different plans to find what works best. That means we must accept that the responsibility for the plan working lies in our control. It is completely dependent upon our accountability to the practice. We must, as a part of our daily practice, be aware of what is working and not working. This will take some time, and we have to be just as diligent (if not more so) in listening to the cues we are given as we are practicing. We may not be able to notice a difference in a day or even a week, but our body, mind, soul, and emotions will give us clues to what works. Journaling (keeping a running log or a meditation journal, for instance) can help track our progress and allow us to see the subtle changes that are taking place. We have to be attentive to the things that make us feel better. We must be willing to manage our existing demands of immediate gratification and be at ease with a more relaxed and long-term gratification that spills into all parts of our life.

So while we might initially think, *Wow, that entire pizza was good; I guess I should eat more pizzas*, we should also be attuned to the realization that when we wake up the next morning after eating an entire pizza, we feel like crap. Noticing what works and what doesn't is an important part of our practice.

We have to assess our progress throughout the plan to notice those feelings and to become proficient at noticing. In running, we assess how we feel after particular runs: Are they too easy or too hard? And how does the process affect our overall health and way of life? We have to try out different times of the day to run, different shoes and clothes, and assess how we feel when running every day versus every other day, how various speeds and distances impact us, and on and on. It is a long-term process with many variables that we need to be aware of and consider. So there is much effort in determining what works and what doesn't, but it's critical that we understand this part of the process.

We have to decide, in many instances, by nothing more than trial and error, which of the many tools is best suited for us and how to practice so we can improve. Again, evaluation of the process is significant, as practicing the wrong way can do more harm than good. For instance, a golfer who's got a technical hitch in her form won't substantially improve until she corrects the form and then practices the correct form over and over. Practicing with poor form may cause the golfer to get better as the body compensates for the poor form, but she'll probably struggle to do so. In the long run she may even get injured and have to quit golf altogether.

By noticing what works, we'll know what to do more of. By doing more of a thing that works, we build confidence in ourselves and in the function of the process. If we start to notice that we feel better following a morning run or a morning meditation, then we should do more of that. The neat thing that happens is not only will there be the immediate feedback of feeling better from the running or meditation; we'll also feel better from having the discipline to practice. There is a great confidence that will build from the discipline we exercise in the practice and from noticing that it works. We have to know that we are unique and that what practices work for someone else may not work for us. We have to recognize our feelings and how we manage to control them, and then we can modify the plan accordingly.

Too often we look for some grand expression of success and become frustrated if we don't see it in our time frame. Be gentle and patient in this process, work on self-awareness, and trust the course of action will provide results. Be open to whatever form those results come in and however they may look.

Enjoy the Ride

Gains will come, but they will be gradual and maybe not in the form we're expecting (as ye sow, so shall ye reap, but you may reap in another field). In some instances we may seem to plateau, so we have to allow ourselves to enjoy the process, by taking solace in the journey itself and how far we've come. Then we can evaluate how we continue forward.

This evaluation will help us notice progress in a broader sense too. We may notice that after the morning meditations we're kinder in our interactions with others, or the drive into work is more pleasant. Each of these progressions is a part of enjoying the journey and part of the larger process of God Confidence. The field you reap in becomes much larger than the one you sow. There is also something to be said for doing good things for ourselves and enjoying the immediate benefit of feeling better all day. Subsequently, we start seeing larger evidence of the difference that is being made in our lives and how this all leads to confidence. And confidence leads to a belief that the practice is working and that leads to more practice and a desire to be more attentive to the signs of what works and what doesn't.

When we do that, we'll start enjoying the ride, seeing the benefits along the way and becoming more accountable and grateful for the daily effort. That effort helps refine the practice, which enhances and speeds the results. And now we have even more confidence, more practice, and more God Confidence.

From a running perspective, you have to enjoy the practice and process of running, such as taking pleasure in being outside, smelling the fresh air, and seeing the color of the horizon change as the sun rises. We can also give thanks for the ability to be out on our run, even though it may not feel like that particular run is making us faster or helping us run longer. So trust that the process will work, but also enjoy the process itself.

Have Faith in the Process

Running is a game of subtle progress, potentially difficult and frustrating at first, and then solid gains become possible. More speed, easier runs at faster paces and longer distances—then a plateau and even a feeling of some backsliding. And the doubtful thoughts begin to creep in, such as "I'm not doing it right," "I'm not doing enough," or "I'm doing too much." That's when it so important to trust and have patience and faith in the process. Just when it seems silliest to trust, we must have confidence in the process.

The process says if I'm not seeing the results I expect then I need to evaluate what's going on. So how do I feel when I run, both physically and mentally? If I notice that I'm really mentally tired then I can switch up the workouts, find a different route, or whatever. If I notice physical tiredness or persistent niggles, I can back off the mileage a bit, take an extra rest day, or get more sleep. However, if it feels good, then I can keep at it.

That's the process: practice, notice your feelings, adjust when necessary, and enjoy your practice even more. It works, and it has worked for everyone who's really tried it since the beginning of time. Also, when the doubts creep in—and they will for a while, as we're exercising years of thinking that run contrary to what we're going to try—remember it is normal to have doubt; but stick with it, it works. So if you're not experiencing some doubt, you're either really superior, in which case you're probably already doing some of this, or you're not trying hard enough.

When the doubts come, that's the most important time to find joy in the process. When I start to feel doubts about how my running is progressing, I force myself to focus on the singular act of the joy of the run. While slogging out ten miles at 5:30 a.m. when it's 12 degrees outside may not sound like there could be any joy in Mudville, find the joy anyway!

For example, notice how there is peace, utter peace outside. Be aware of the sound of your feet (when writing this I actually typed "feat" instead of "feet," and I laughed, as it really is the sound of both that keeps you going) and your dog's paws passing over the pavement in what, if you really pay attention, is an effortless flow of life and energy that moves the miles by. Find the joy; the majesty in the sky, the brilliance of the stars in the dark sky reminding you of the power and immensity of the universe, and know that this power is also in you. And finally, revel in the joy of finishing, and knowing a warm shower and breakfast awaits you.

The same is true of the daily ways: practice, enjoy, and trust. This will keep you going, as sometimes the progress is small, and we have to be very aware to notice the benefit. Sometimes we're looking for the big bang, as it were, but we can also notice the small things because there is joy, celebration, and gratitude in that practice, and it will lead to more. And notice, because not noticing or not enjoying the daily independent practice causes some to stop short, and that will always leave you with a sense of *what if* …

Establish Some Goals

Running takes nothing more than waking, lacing up the shoes, and going. Establishing goals around running and making it a routine, a process and a habit makes running more interesting. It also provides you with a sense of measure, accomplishment, and a lasting physical and emotional health benefit.

Building a God Confident life takes nothing more than waking, following some specific practices, and being. As with running, establishing goals around God Confidence, making it a routine, and evaluating progress makes the whole process more interesting and provides a sense of accomplishment. It also provides lasting physical and emotional health benefits.

In running, if you log the miles, you will be able to run farther; if you run faster for certain periods, you will be able to run faster for longer distances; and you'll begin to reap the physical and mental benefits. In the quest for God Confidence, if you establish a daily practice, you will have more connection with God. If you do that multiple times a day, or have varied practices, you will establish the connection for longer periods of time, and you'll begin to reap the physical and emotional benefits more quickly.

Regardless of your objectives, if you state them in writing, build a plan to achieve them, and then execute that plan, you'll get and be better even if you don't always hit the target. For instance, when running, you can just go out and run, enjoying the benefits of being outside, exercising, and having fun. You'll notice some benefits and feel good—there is nothing wrong with that. Additionally, though, you can establish specific goals around running, determine the training plan necessary to meet those goals, and begin. This approach allows you to enjoy, feel good, and have some measure of your progress, and you'll have an ultimate goal to shoot for.

So, as a runner, you decide that you're going to run a marathon (or a half marathon, 10k, 5k, ultra marathon, whatever the distance) in a certain time. You do some research and come up with a number of training plans and approaches to meet that goal. You select the one that works best for your schedule and running style, and you're off. In general, these plans will call for a certain number of miles to be run each week, for a certain number of weeks, based on the distance of the race you're aspiring to complete. The mileage will be split between easy, longer runs; shorter, faster training runs; maybe some cross training; some hill work; and some rest days. So for any particular day during a training plan you'll know what's expected based on the plan. Week by week you can track your progress, according to plan. You evaluate whether you're able to complete the mileage easily, whether the times are faster or slower than the plan calls for, and determine if your physical and mental health is meeting your running needs.

Again, much like running, you'll find establishing a God Confidence practice will take physical and mental conditioning. When you are executing a running plan there will be days when doing what's on the plan truly seems daunting. Sometimes nasty weather will seem like a godsend—*ahhh*, a real excuse to not run even though the plan calls for a run. Other times you'll just say you're tired, or your legs hurt (this is not to say that you should ignore injury or truly tired legs; that may dictate a change to the plan like doing an easy short run vs. speed session, but we all know the difference), or you have to be to work early, or whatever excuse you can come up with to not lace up the treads. However, those days will come back to haunt you. Mentally, it will start to weigh on you. It will feed the doubt that is always lurking under the surface that says you really can't achieve the goal. That mental struggle is tiring, and it will deplete your energy. It will grow from skipping a run to cutting mileage or time on another, and so the downward spiral begins as the physical implications of the plan cutting start to mount.

On the other hand, you can establish an upward spiral to your training runs. You rejoice in the opportunity to be able to run, you find the aliveness in being outside, exercising your body and building fitness, health and mental fortitude. Each time you complete a run, you overcome an obstacle and can rejoice in the fact that you ran. You will build confidence in the process and in your ability ... just like with practicing to establish God Confidence. Your runs will be easier, you'll start to see consistent time improvements, and you'll build a stronger and more habitual practice. I can honestly say I've had to deal with lament and woe about not running (I saw it somewhere that there is nothing more motivating than the thought of having to put "0 miles" in your running log), but I have never finished a run and said I wish I'd not done that today. Maybe it's the runner's high, but I think it is more a condition of living in a certain way, and running supports the emotional and physical way of being that always feels good.

The other thing that will happen is if you follow the plan and put in the miles: You will achieve your goals. Whether it is to finish, or finish in a specific time, you will make it. Maybe not on the first try, but it will happen. Running is practice and commitment, and like any endeavor, when you practice and keep at it, you will get better. There will be times when you do everything right and don't meet your goal, but you will be closer than you were when you started. There is always another race and an opportunity to try again, and you have enjoyed the process of getting to where you are.

God Confidence is no different. You establish goals, you practice, and you will ultimately meet your goals. While it may not happen the first time, and maybe not all the time, you will be closer. There is always another opportunity, and you have enjoyed the process of getting to where you are.

Daily Ways

What follows are some tools, techniques, and practices that one can do to begin to establish a personal relationship with God, and ultimately a God Confident life. These items can be done alone or in combination with others. I'd suggest that you select either one or just a few that make sense and fit into your world at this time. As you go along, feel free to change it up, drop some, and add others, but give them your dedication and time and observe how they make you feel. They say it takes twenty-one days to create a new habit, so it would be good to commit yourself to at least three weeks of practicing the ones you pick.

It is not recommended to try them all at once, as it could be overwhelming and hard to evaluate what's working and what's not. In any event, look at the tools, think about your goals, and then outline how you'll begin practicing, and which tools you'll use when. Enjoy the process each and every day, as enjoyment is the key to success. Set both long and short-term goals, and large and small goals, and oh yeah—enjoy.

Observational Perceptive Connection: OPC

One strategy in establishing God Confidence can be practicing Observational Perceptive Connection (OPC). I'm fairly confident it's not a clinical term, but it is meaningful for the practice of God Confidence. All too often we look through others or past them in the hectic pace of the day-to-day activities of the outside world. OPC suggests that we observe someone, not just look mindlessly at them, but really connect with them. In other words, consider what they are really about. Take just an instant to really look at and feel someone and perceive their being. Consider their actions, words, thoughts, energy, and their whole spirit. Do this not to evaluate or to judge, but to perceive their nature and their story.

We all have stories. We all have the stories of our lives, from a combination of childhood memories, formative events, and the influences of friends, careers, and families. All of that forms who we are; it then drives our actions at a macro level, which fuels the day-to-day behaviors of our current actions. Thus, everyone is operating from the basis of their story or their history. OPC asks us to perceive that story and consider that their actions are not solely in-the-moment decisions made to either impress us or piss us off.

Rather, their actions are based on a body of life experience that is greater than just this moment. Thus, the objective of OPC is to experience the person beyond the story. We do that by first accepting that they have a story that's driving them, just as we have one that drives us. Empathy, compassion, and patience for others are the benefits that come from OPC. The perspective that accepts they are working from a broad and deep story that we don't know allows us to not take things so personally and to really experience another person for their being rather than for their story. It also helps us consider that we too are more than our story, to begin to understand how our story drives our habits and actions, and to determine how we'd like to adapt ourselves.

To begin to practice OPC, we have to break the cycle of action/reaction. We have to find a way to interpret our reaction to someone cutting us off in traffic, or making a rude remark, or whatever may set us off. We can begin by taking the time to understand that they are operating from some story that goes beyond just this moment. We do this not for the purpose of judgment, or for the purpose of excusing poor behavior, or to try to think we *know* someone. We do this merely for the purpose of reminding ourselves how much they are like us. We want to build a connection, even if it is temporary.

We also accept that they are on a path that has twists and turns that have gotten them to where they are today, to the action that has linked us together. And whether we appreciate that action in this moment or not, we can, hopefully, appreciate that they are spiritual beings experiencing the human realm. Understanding that they have a story allows us to pause our reaction, to break the cycle of judgment of the person and the situation, and allows us to develop a personal connection with them. Once we've done that it becomes much easier to relax into whatever the situation is. Thinking about someone else's story reminds us that we have a story too, and that commonality establishes a connection. Just knowing a story builds a relationship, and that can be enjoyed as a connection with another, no matter how real the story. The connection is energetic, it is real, it is compassionate, and it is God!

A key component here is to remember that the story isn't what is important. It is the practice of making a connection with another. The practice is becoming acquainted with another's energy by observing them. Next, you build a perception based not on the immediate event that brought you together, but on a connection of likeness: Everyone has a story, so we are all the same. We all operate from a model that is based on habits formed by our story. So if we are able to break the reactive cycle of our own habits and story, we have a chance to make a different connection. With this practice we begin to move from making a judgment based off the story to building a connection with another.

It is a catch-and-release program of sorts, where we catch a human moment, center it to build/establish an energetic connection, then release any judgment and negative energy we started to build. This process allows us to begin to relate to people as other creations of God just like us, rather than actors in a particular circumstance that we've been conditioned to immediately evaluate as good or bad. This process not only helps us get over those spikes of disdain, anger, and the like, but it also helps us to understand and practice releasing feelings and thoughts, and to not become attached to any stories, particularly our own. This process allows our judgmental tendencies to relax, ease, and dissipate.

Nonsituational Dependence: NSD

This is another strategy that I'm fairly sure is not a clinical concept. In any event, the idea is that we approach events from the inside out rather than from the outside in. We are not dependent on the situation to determine our feelings or actions. It is all too easy to get caught up in a situation or circumstance and allow that event to shape our feelings, and not just for the duration of the event, but for minutes, hours, days, or even longer afterward.

How many times has someone asked us why we look upset or unhappy, and our response is "we're having a bad day"? In most instances, that feeling of having a bad day is manifested because something happened earlier in the day that got us off on the wrong foot, or "it's just one thing after another" that has us down. We react to the events around us; we get upset when something goes wrong or excited when something goes right.

Practicing NSD means we can begin to experience owning our feelings and reactions, rather than allowing them to be dependent on the situation. We don't have to hide or suppress our reactions or feelings when a situation makes us feel a certain way. However, we can and should keep the feelings confined to just that situation. We can respect that while we may feel sad or mad or glad, it is a temporary state based on us, not on the circumstance we are experiencing in that moment. Moments/experiences come and go, and we have to be able to establish our basic orientation to that flow of life. That orientation can be rooted in our being, or at the whims of the events and circumstances we experience. Working on establishing NSD supports a way of being that is controlled by us and has a core in peace. Without that, we are subjected to roller coaster–like reactions to the events around us that we judgmentally deem either good or bad.

Too often, we carry the baggage of loss or disappointment or anger with us for extended periods. We've all heard to not "bring the office home with us." In other words, don't let the activity and events of the day taint interactions with others that are in no way connected to those events. When we've experienced some type of dysfunction that we allow to eat away at us, we are usually compelled to retell "what happened to me" over and over. The event is singular and fleeting, but retold time and time again it lives on with us. It is as if we can't get enough of the emotion of the event, so we have a need to share our perception of it repeatedly in an addictive sense so we can relive our upset.

There is a story of two monks that came upon a woman having difficulty crossing a small stream, and the older of the two monks helped her across. The woman offered no thanks or recognition of the aid and even had an air of rudeness about her. A while later as the monks continued along their way, the younger of the two asked why the women had been so rude as to not offer gratitude for the help, and why the older monk had not said anything about it at the time. The older monk simply replied. "I put that women down hours ago, why are you still carrying her?" How often do we carry things with us that happened hours, days, or even years ago? The event won't ever change, but we always can. We carry things with us to the point that it becomes our story. While there is nothing wrong with sharing the events of our day with others or our history with those close to us, it is problematic if we relive them so vividly that the emotion returns and is allowed to taint the present moment and the relationship we're experiencing in that moment. Building a gap allows us to get in between the event and our being and emotions.

Over time we'll begin to create a habitual frame for our feelings and our state of being. We do this by moving from the immediate emotion and reaction of an event to a gap. The gap is built by thinking about the story or building a story (OPC). Once we've broken the reactive and emotional cycle with a connection to another (OPC) we can then focus on our being in that moment. We can experience that event in a manner that realizes the event is a point in time that has a human feeling attached to it, but is also temporary. Once we accept the temporary nature of a particular circumstance we can base our feeling and state of being on our core. This is who we are all the time, and not just what we experienced in the heat of the moment. We get to a state of NSD that is the state of peace. Practiced diligently, it leads to God Confidence.

NSD then allows us to experience events and not be ruled by the situation, whether they are happy or sad. We want to get to a point where we are in peace and joy regardless of the situation. Not numb, but fully alive in the experience and, most importantly, in ourselves, our spirit, and in all endeavors.

Gratitude

Being thankful is such a receptive state for spirit. It covers a number of bases. Gratitude assumes awareness. To say *thank you* means I'm aware of something being done for me. We most often think of gratitude as saying thank you to God for something. However, I don't want to discount the daily thanks we say to others in the course of our daily action. We hear *thank you* a lot for a kind word, the holding of a door, or assistance with a task. So that form of gratitude counts, because what we're going for here is an acknowledgment of the world around us working for us, through others, ourselves, and of course, God.

This acknowledgment is a part of the practice that supports our building of God Confidence. It is a knowing and a participation in a world that is good to us and provides assistance (large and small) in so many ways. Like so many things that happen every day, thanksgiving can become almost rote, an automatic but thoughtless response. Let's not take our thanksgiving for granted and just spout it out as a conditioned response to any action for another. We've even come to the point where our gratitude is a form of sarcasm—as in *thanks!* And how often do we automatically type *Thanks* as a salutation of an e-mail when the content is merely informational and not requesting any assistance from the recipient. *Thanks* has become a form of business pleasantry in instances where it may not be warranted. But words mean things, and to be sincere they have to be given meaning in the correct context.

To have meaning requires intention on either the part of the sender or the receiver, and to have intention requires awareness and deliberate intent. So if we must append *thank you* to any and all correspondence, or if it is an automatic response for us, let us practice the process of "thank you" from the heart, in a way that we thoughtfully choose. We need to make sure that we are aware of the energy around the words coming out of our mouth. We should be aware of whatever gratitude we express, and aware of what sparks that gratitude.

You see, something spawns the words "thank you" to leave our lips. We need to be really conscious of when and how we use the words, as this awareness will lead to a greater understanding of the things that create the feeling of *thank you*. Subsequently, we'll train ourselves to be aware of just the feeling, and we'll notice that feeling is really with us a lot more than we ever imagined, and ultimately it will be with us always—and really is with us always. We just have to allow ourselves to experience it and express it thoughtfully and with purpose.

Thanksgiving for Past, Present, and Future

Getting back to our initial thought about gratitude and giving thanks to God, there are different time frames for us to consider when we are practicing gratitude. Mary Morrissey describes the gratitude time frames in *Prosperity Plus—A New Way Of Living* as past, present, and future.

Past gratitude is the most common. Saying thanks for something I've already received or have, such as thanks for the great test score, thanks for the safe trip, thanks for the good day, and so on.

Present gratitude is thanks for the moment, the food before us, the awakening in the morning, the breath of life. It is thanks for helping the car stop before running through a stop sign, or thanks for the five bucks lying in the parking lot.

Future gratitude is thanks for what will come to be, or thanks for things not currently in form. This can be difficult, because with past and present gratitude, the thing we are thankful for already happened or is happening. It is usually in a material form, and we can see, hold, and experience it. But future gratitude can seem more like wishing than thanksgiving. But we have to remember that everything is energy, and when we are putting out a vibration of thanksgiving, we are really making things welcome. These are things that may not have materialized yet, but by welcoming them, by approaching them with an attitude of thanksgiving, we are positioning ourselves to be in a receiving state. We receive what we think about, give energy too—give thanks for. In Matthew 21:22 this concept is explained. "If you believe, you will receive whatever you ask for in prayer." And perhaps the more well-known verse in Matthew 7:7 supports the idea of answered prayers even more: "Ask and it will be given to you; seek and you will find; knock and the door will be opened to you."

Both of these verses highlight the energetic nature of the universe and the necessity to believe and to act confidently. Great faith is no accident; it comes from a consistent practice with the energy and laws of the universe and an awareness of the successes of that practice. If you are genuine, consistent, and aware, you will come to realize the power of those verses and the power of prayer and thanksgiving. However, if you say the thanksgiving prayer for the future thing, but in your mind you don't believe you will receive it, your thoughts will cancel out your words.

Being grateful is also much more than just saying *thank you*; it is really a process of living. It is not just saying *thanks* but living thanks. And how do we live thanks? We enjoy life. Part of any gratitude practice is enjoying what you have, being grateful for the small things, and really loving your world and your stuff. As the Sheryl Crow song *Soak up the Sun* goes, "it's not having what you want, but wanting what you got." How true, as that is living gratitude and thanksgiving. Living thanks is also living fully, in God Confidence, with an eye toward generosity. The fact that we are participating in the circulation and flow of the universe is at the very heart of the concept of gratitude, and being a joyous and a beneficial presence is how we genuinely *live* thank you.

Actions speak louder than words, so if you really want to say thank you, show how thankful you are by living in God Confidence: Live thank you. When a child gets a gift, what's the best thank you one can get? The forced *thank you* that comes only at the bequest of the parent, or the excitement in the youngster's eyes, a squeal of delight, and the hours of adventure and joy that the child gains from the gift? Obviously it's the latter—and our lives in the eyes of the infinite, and our own hearts are no different. True thanks are not expressed by a "thank you" through gritted teeth. It is tithing, volunteering, and living and receiving with a light and joyous heart and spirit. It is appreciating the beauty in nature, in small things, in all things. It is living in a way that demonstrates how lucky we are to have this life, whatever it might hold for us, all the while knowing it a gift that is ours to live as we choose.

How do we position ourselves to get more gifts, more of what we want, more happiness, abundance, and love? It is not done by smiling and squeaking out a forced "thank you" because we know we need to. While the gift may not be exactly what we were hoping for, we get closer to what we do want by living with excitement in our eyes and joy with the gift that has been given. We begin to feel this gratitude with focus on the giver rather than the gift. We consider that the giver has made effort on our behalf and has been thoughtful in their mind and heart and given us a gift. We can also realize that all gifts ultimately come from God through the giver. It is now our opportunity to experience that gift—experience it not from the material perspective of how we'll use it, but rather from the spiritual perspective of the gift being an example of love and joy. That is truly the gift of life, and living with feeling, with joy, and exuberance demonstrates thanks—and that demonstration is the process of really living thanks.

Every day I say thank you for this body that carries me and for the fitness and health that allows me to move freely. When I run, I demonstrate my joy and gratitude for that health and fitness. Not every run is what I've hoped for and not every goal is met, but I still run with joy. I take consolation in knowing that while the goal that I was aware of may not have been met, some greater goal was.

So often the focus is just on the specific prize, and we lose sight of the fact that the universe is always plotting for our good. In that vein, there may be gifts we get that we are not aware of, but they are gifts nonetheless. We don't need to know what the gift is, simply that there is one. That is a key part of living thanks and God Confidence: being secure in knowing each and every day we are provided for and receiving exactly what we need. We know that our living thanks and giving thanks, regardless of the circumstances, will allow us to not only be aware of the gift, but also make welcome bigger and better gifts. We can then attract gifts that are perfect for us, as they are our own creation, our own idea of the best gift: gifts that we give to ourselves as we practice God Confidence and building an amazing life.

Visioning the Day, Fulfilling Your Dreams

Part of any successful activity is preparation and planning. From a running perspective, it is important to know what you hope to achieve from a given run. Understanding those goals prepares me to be able to run for the particular purpose, and enjoy the run for what it is. This preparation allows a mental focus: Right before the run I gear up for whatever type of workout I'm going to be dealing with, and I start to envision the run.

Additionally, there is longer-term planning involved in the process as I map out my runs for the week. Even longer-term plans may include ramping up for races and developing a schedule to be sure that I'm ready for the races I want to complete. For example, I have a long-term goal of running a marathon in all fifty states, so I plan out each year for the races I'd like to run, and then I plan my weekly running schedule based on the race calendar and what the particular week and every day calls for (long run, recovery run, rest day, etc.).

As was mentioned in chapter 2, "Sports as Divine," visualization is a huge part of almost any performance activity: seeing the ball go into the hole, sticking the landing, winning the game, winning a championship. Whatever the activity, there are pictures associated with our definition of personal and group success. Those pictures create emotions (or maybe the emotions are there, just behind the veil of awareness, and they actually create the pictures). Those emotions anchor our feeling and contribute to our successful behavior. So our day and our dream are no different; we have a long-term goal with short-term objectives that move us toward that goal. Thus, a key practice in learning (remembering) how to live our daily lives in God Confidence is to start each day by visioning how that day will go, based on what we have going on and our objectives for that day.

The idea of visioning big things is not uncommon to any of us, as we've all daydreamed at one time or another. We've all thought about our perfect scene: the successful career, perfect partner, perfect body, dream home … *ahhh*, nirvana. The reason we don't recognize that as a visioning practice is that we don't practice it. We do it as a distraction from the "real world" and write it off as wishful thinking. However, it is that very thinking that will create our real world. It just needs to be defined, focused and practiced in the same manner one practices a sport, music, or any activity where we hope to improve our performance and results. We establish the goal, lay out the plan, and practice to get good enough to achieve it.

The practice is really the key aspect, and one of the quickest ways to make the practice a habit is to do it on a daily basis. And a good starting point is to begin every day by thinking about how that particular day will look.

Anchoring the Vision for the Day

I start each day by running through pictures of what the perfect day will look like for me, and I usually do that within the context of thanksgiving. So it starts with: *Thank you, God, for waking me this morning and keeping me awake throughout the day. Thank you for a relaxed and easy morning of getting ready for work, the chores done, and the girls ready for school. Thank you for safe travels to work, school, and errands, and for easy, efficient and close parking at work, the store, wherever.* (Yes, being thankful for the small things like finding good parking is how we start to get into the flow of gratitude and the appreciation for all things.) Subsequently, we make welcome the small and large alike. I then give thanks for a good day at work, effective communication with my team, peers, and clients, and access to the wisdom of the infinite to deal with whatever circumstances may come my way. Thanks for the laughter of the day and safe travel home, for an enjoyable and relaxing evening with the family, filled with joy, laughter, and realization of our love for each other.

That's the generic version. If I've got specific stuff in a particular day—a big meeting, presentation, or difficult conversation—I craft the vision more specifically. But I keep the focus on connection to the infinite and being relaxed and enjoying the day (Remember Eckhart Tolle's words about enjoying being " in joy in oneself").

This can also be done throughout the course of the day as things come up or plans get changed. The opportunity to express our intentions can be done at any time.

Anchoring the Dream

In addition to visioning a good day, I also work on "seeing" and "feeling" my longer-term dream or vision. This vision is whatever big thing you desire to achieve, or whatever you want your world to look like. For me, it is the message in this book and the subsequent promotion of the idea of God Confidence. Every day starts and ends the same way, with a dream. The dream is a visualization of what I want my life to look like. I imagine what I will be doing to promote the message and how it will grow. I have pictures I run through of how my days will look, what I'll do and with whom I'll associate. Most importantly, I envision how God Confidence will move people to action in their own lives, and the joy and power that will come to people as they establish a deep, personal relationship with God. Even better, I think of how those relationships will ripple through their families, their communities, and ultimately change the perspective of the world. Or at least their perspective of the world ... but isn't that the same thing?

Part of God Confidence is a feeling and a knowing that you're heading in the right direction, confident that you are making it happen, and confident that you can be close to God no matter what your circumstance or point on the path is right now. A vision does not have to be grandiose, nor does it have to be limited in scope or concept. It can change and grow just as we change and grow, so don't hold back or think your thoughts are too big or too small. Think them and feel into them and *notice* when they manifest, both the big and the small.

Too often we dream big dreams and expect them to happen in accordance with our time frame and then lose sight, focus, and confidence when we don't see it all manifest just as we envisioned. The gardener prepares the soil, plants the seeds, pulls the weeds, waters, and waits. The gardener does all the things to make welcome the coming plant from the seed, but can do nothing to speed that process. And impatiently digging up the seed to see if it's growing is obviously counterproductive. The gardener must have faith that the seed will grow, as God has designed it to.

So too with our dreams: We do everything we can to make our dreams welcome, but we don't dictate the time it will take to manifest. Remember, this is about a process, and as we establish a relationship with God we build confidence, and that confidence will allow us to accept the universe's time frame rather than our own. It will allow us to celebrate the joy of participating in the process of building our lives, and experience joy in the moment we are in, no matter what that looks like.

The enjoyment of the process means we notice what is going on around us, not just focusing exclusively on whether or not we've achieved our dream. When we notice the small things that are coming into being we begin to see things in a conceptual form and a process. We attune ourselves to seeing the evolution of the concept, not just a final concrete product. That can be such a challenge, because as we get more comfortable with God (read: more comfortable with ourselves as divine beings), we get excited, and that excitement can lead to grand visions that we may not be ready for just yet. The mind can think big things, and it must, and the soul can feel great things, and it must, but they are not always in sync from a timing perspective. So we have to be patient and enjoy where we are before we go on. It really is about the journey and not just the destination.

When I first started working on this process of visioning, one of the things I routinely envisioned was being relaxed and at ease with the world around me so that I could choose my actions and be deliberate in my decision making. What happened? Nothing, or at least that's what I thought. I saw myself getting agitated and feeling frustrated, and thinking only after the fact that I could have made a different decision. *However,* what I started to notice was that at least I was noticing. I was now aware of the agitated feeling and that I had other options when it came to choices I made … *hmmm* … could this be progress? I certainly never had those thoughts before, so I decided to work on becoming more aware of not just the events of the day, but also on my process of going through those events. What I started to see was, at a conceptual level, what I'd been visioning. It wasn't exactly a relaxed and deliberate management of my feelings and actions, but it was close. It was an awareness of the process of what I wanted and a step to get to what I wanted. It was progress toward the vision.

The real validation of the progress came in the form of a family vacation we took a couple of years back. We always have fun together, but as with any group of four people (plus a Chihuahua, and enough provisions for a month-long trip instead of a week of vacation) in tight confines over an extended period, there is usually an inevitable fly in the ointment. Someone gets sick or tired or sick and tired or you have to wait too long to find a restroom or the food is bad or you can't sleep or you get caught in traffic or—you get the picture. Something always seems to trigger moments (or several) of strife, and sometimes that discord becomes a lot bigger than it needs to be.

But *this* vacation was different! Everyone was happy, got along together, was cooperative, all the things we wanted to do fell into place, the kids got the playtime they needed, and the adults got their time to commiserate with friends. It was smooth, even when we got stuck in traffic just a few miles from our hotel late one evening. While we were all tired and grumpy and wanted to be at the hotel, it never escalated. It was like we were all aware of what a roll we were on, and we were not going to let this little blip derail us. Again, all of that could have gone unnoticed, but I was training myself to pay attention.

As I was establishing a closer relationship with God, I was seeing my power. I was beginning to understand how broad the connection with God is, in that it extended beyond just the things I was specific about—the content—but to the larger concepts I was longing for.

So the message in all that is to be aware of all the stuff that is going on, not just how close or far you are from the specific content of the vision. Keep the ultimate goal in mind, of course, and evaluate your progress nonjudgmentally. Also allow yourself the ancillary rewards that are the normal and natural by-products of God Confidence … it all just feels better.

Also, don't dismiss or discount feeling better, because as Abraham has said via Jerry and Ester Hicks: It is all about vibrations, and the higher our levels of vibration, the more in tune we are to greater levels of becoming, and we have to be vibrating at a level that is harmonious with what we want. So enjoy and rejoice in vibrating at a higher level because that is how we ultimately establish God Confidence.

Build an initial relationship with God and yourself while pursuing your dream and that relationship will result in better feelings and events, and thus a higher vibration. That higher vibration will allow a deepening of your relationship with God, which allows for yet a higher vibration and so you create an ever-upward spiral. So keep feeling good, vision your day and your dream, and NOTICE.

Affirmations

Simply, affirmations are phrases that allow you to verbalize a positive idea about a particular topic. In the Saturday Night Live skit, I'm good enough, smart enough, and doggone it, people like me. While that was very tongue-in-cheek, if you put aside your preconceived notions about affirmations and just say that out loud, you cannot help but to feel just a little bit better about yourself. And even if you won't let that help you feel better, there is still the energy of the positive statement that moves us to a better place, even if we may not feel it for ourselves. The universe (God) does hear it and feel it and begin to act upon it.

In our Unity services, as we prepare for meditation, we sometimes sing a song that has a line in it that says, "our thoughts are prayers and we are always praying." The point is that our thoughts count too in the art of affirmations. As I have mentioned before, if we are saying one thing but thinking another, our thoughts can counteract our words. Our thoughts also affect our feelings, so be careful what you think of. If your overall feeling is unfavorable, then you can be sure that your thoughts are in the negative realm, or at a lower vibration. So while saying the positive affirmation is the first step, getting your thoughts in line with it will make your efforts more effective.

A lot of spiritual literature (and secular literature for that matter) talks about how words mean things, which impacts us and others, and that they have an energy associated with them that could either be uplifting or degrading. And while we've all heard, "sticks and stones may break my bones but words can never hurt me" (perhaps everyone's earliest affirmation), we usually say that to ourselves in the midst of tears that have come from someone saying a hateful, hurtful thing to us, in an attempt to make ourselves feel better.

Clearly we know and feel that words can and do have an impact. Unfortunately, like with so many things today, it seems we often take the negative to heart and ignore or downplay the positive. Why do we allow the vitriol of hate speech or other negative talk to make us feel bad, to feel attacked by the words, and yet affirmations are seen as an airy-fairy escape tactic from the real world? Do we feel that the practicality, harsh reality, and truth of the world we live in dictate that things and people are unfair and mean, and thus we've accepted the power of the negative? Is it merely experience based on years of examples that formulates our perspective?

In any event, I'm sure we've all felt the sting of an unkind word, slur, or put down. So if we know that a bad word can produce a bad feeling, why not accept, embrace, and establish new experiential examples of good words producing good feelings? Let's begin to allow ourselves the experience of positive statements—affirmations—creating positive, kind, and uplifting feelings. This includes the words we direct at others, as well as words we aim at ourselves (also known as self-talk).

Words mean things. They have a powerful impact, so let's choose to use kind words. Let's choose to have those words direct us in our aspirations and in the joy of the everyday. Think of it this way: The words we say have energy, and since energy never dies, our words are floating around in the ether forever. We can never take them back. So what kind of words do you want to have floating around out there?

Much like I mentioned in the three Rs, the more specific the replacement thought can be, the more power it has, and so too with affirmations. The more specific the affirmation is to the context at hand, the more powerful its effect will be. So feel free to make up your own affirmations that have to do with the specific thought or feeling you want to have. I want to be a happier, better person, so one of my daily affirmations is "I am joyous, generous, and grateful." Whatever the context of the affirmation, there is a lot of power in the "I am" statement, claiming not just "I want to be" or "I'd like to have," but that you *are* and you *have*.

Other than that, I don't have a lot of guidance on how to phrase your affirmations. There are lots of writings, discussions, and books on affirmations, so if you don't like the idea of coming up with your own, find some and make them your own. One such book I'll mention because of the specificity and powerful affirmations it contains is Louise Hay's *You Can Heal Your Life*. While this book is broader than just affirmations, it contains a litany of affirmations specific to any number of mental and physical health challenges. There's no need to make up your own if you're at a loss for words. The book also provides some great real-life examples of the power of affirmations.

It bears repeating: The key really is that words mean things. If you say words with the conviction, feeling, and believing that they are true, they do great things. We've all seen and experienced the power of words to do harm and inflict pain, so let's establish a new experience by using affirmations daily for ourselves and others. If you still think saying an affirmation is hokey, the great thing about it is you can say it to yourself and no one else knows, just you. That way you save face and still reap the benefits of the affirmation.

I'd argue, though, that the greatest gift you can give yourself and others is the gift of using language to make the world a better place. Kind words are spawned by kind thoughts, and they spawn kind action. Start the experience of letting folks see the power of kind words by affirming the kindness in you with daily affirmations.

Daily Meditation/Prayer/Contemplation

Probably the most powerful, specific, and habit-forming act that we can do is the practice of daily meditation, prayer, and/or quiet contemplation. Much like I've used the term God to denote any and all forms of higher power regardless of the name used, meditation, prayer, and contemplation are terms for the general concept of being still and devoting time to something larger than yourself.

So whatever you call it, allow yourself to spend time in the silence with God on a daily basis. It has been said, "if prayer is when we talk to God, meditation is when we listen." Again, I don't want to get caught up in the terms or the technical processes. I just want everyone to devote some time each day to be with God. I can say from experience that it is truly transformative. We are always with God, but for some time each day we should *be* with God in a focused and deliberate way. The intention of being still, quiet, and devoting time specifically to that purpose is powerful. It is effective from both the perspective of making (or allowing) contact with a higher power, but also in the practice of devoting time with specific intention, and practicing that process on a daily basis.

So many benefits can result from meditation, including reduced stress, mental clarity, calmer demeanor, and so on. But perhaps the most broadly significant benefit is the fact that meditation is a practice that requires practice, and the will to complete and establish it as a habit and to hone and refine our individual practice is very constructive for us. What more powerful skill is there to have than to be able to train yourself to devote time to a thing with deliberate intent and make it habitual? That skill applies to every action and process we take part in, from work to relationships to play and to spiritual expression. Much like affirmations, there are a good number of great books and CDs on the process of meditation. Pick one up and find a process that works for you. Or go to a meditation center and participate. In whatever form and method you choose, you can't go wrong with any type of meditation.

Minute Meditations

Most everyone thinks about time, but few of us are aware of time and really notice when we are noticing it. When we do notice time, it is usually in the context of lack: we're late for something, or we think we don't have enough time. But how often do we notice time in the context of abundance, when time stands still, when the moment captures us, when we have more than enough time (always) and notice the enjoyment in taking our time? There is immense power in approaching things from the perspective of abundance.

We notice time every day with appointments, reminders on our phones and computers, schedules, meetings, calls, and general demands for our time throughout the day. With all of this noticing of time, we can also take the opportunity to notice that we need to take time to be with ourselves and to just breathe. It may not feel like we have that luxury at times, and those are the exact moments when it's most important.

I work to be aware of time, and I notice my feelings around time and events that are scheduled. One of my practices to expand time in my daily life is that I try to never set an alarm to get up in the morning. I usually wake up and go for a run, so part of my practice has been to let my waking dictate my runs. If I wake up early, I go for a longer run, and if I sleep later, I go for a shorter run. Normally, my waking is within a thirty- to forty-minute time frame. As I started this practice, I became more aware of how starting my day on my own time left me feeling more relaxed and ready for the day, and more aware of time in the context of abundance—that I have plenty of it.

Now the reality is that there was (and some days still is) a long period where this process felt odd. I felt pressure to wake up at a specific time (still without an alarm) in order to get in the miles my training plan called for that day. And I felt a good deal of frustration if I slept later than I'd planned and had to go for a shorter run. But as this happened I started to accept the flow of the day, telling myself that I must listen to my body and let it tell me when it needed more sleep and when it needed a longer run.

As I surrendered (the word surrender has such a negative connotation, but really, why is doing away with struggle a bad thing?) to the process of not being able to change when I'd awakened, I began to see my day being more about my relationship with the world around me. I began to be more open to the process of life, the natural rhythms of the day, and I was more attuned to being a part of a larger orchestration of time and space. I was less concerned about me (little me) and what I wanted to force on the world, and more about the *me* (big me) that's connected and a part of a natural flow.

Going with the proverbial flow has allowed me to be calmer. As I've continued to work on this process, it has helped me feel that I actually have more time, and I spend it more completely. Not just by accepting the flow of the day and time but by single tasking, focusing on the action of the moment. Accepting this more abundant context of time allows me to be less concerned about what's next and that I may not have enough time, and more concentrated on the now, the moment at hand. Amazingly, when you focus on only one thing, time expands. As anyone new to meditation will tell you, five minutes never seems so long as when all you're trying to do is nothing.

In any event, this noticing of time can be particularly helpful in our daily work and activity. As I noted earlier, most all of us are clock-watchers in some form or another. We are occupied by the questions of time: when is the next meeting, is it time to pick up the kids, will I be late to work, how long until I get off work? There are reminders popping up, in what seems like a constant barrage, of the clock laughing at us.

So let's use that clock watching to our advantage, by taking minute meditations. At some point after the waking and running practice, I started to notice the time on the clock. I began to realize that I'd often look at the clock when all the numbers were the same—11:11, 3:33 and so forth. I began to play with that, and whenever I would look and see all the numbers on the clock matching (1:11, 2:22, 3:33, etc.) I would stop, take a deep breath, and pause in meditation for one minute.

Now, a minute may seem like a really long time, or it may seem like too little time to make a difference. For those that think the minute seems like a really long time, it may feel that way at first, but slowly it will start to seem more comfortable, and finally it will be something where you can't wait for the next hour to experience again. For those that think the minute will be too short, any amount of time is a good amount to pause and be with yourself and God. And you can always do more time. I don't think this practice should be an extended meditation but merely a break in the routine where we can celebrate awareness and talk/listen to God. So two or three minutes is fine, but save your longer meditations for morning and evening, or morning, noon, and night. Use these minute meditations as short and simple opportunities to thoughtfully breathe during the rush of the day and take them for what they are: subtle reminders of our connection and our God Confidence.

Initially, you'll be amazed at how often you notice the times for minute meditations. Also, in addition to the all 1s, 2s, and so on, I also count 6:06, 7:07, 8:08, 9:09, 10:10, and 12:12—so you can do one every hour. Then you'll just smile as you are about to pull out your hair with a challenge on the desk in front of you and you look up at the clock and see 4:44 ... *ahhh*.

Here's my process for minute meditations:

- Notice the time (but don't force it and "plan" around it, as this really defeats the purpose and concept if you set an alarm for these times).
- Take a deep, deliberate breath, feeling the air move in and out of the entire body.
- Tense every muscle at once, as tight as possible, hold for just a second or two, and release.
- Take another deep breath.
- Say thank you for the awareness of this minute.
- Then just sit for a minute.
- Say thank you for the pause, and appreciate that time for God.

Three Rs: Realize, Reflect, Replace

As mentioned in chapter 4, the three Rs can help you change the way you react to events in your life. Awareness of our emotions is a critical step in establishing a God Confident life. A key precept of God Confidence is being in control of how we feel, act, and are. So being able to recognize an emotion and, subsequently, knowing ourselves well enough to know where that feeling will lead is a significant practice for us to build. So much of our fast-paced lives seem to be done on autopilot. We act and react, unaware of the events causing the actions. There are times when it seems as if our reactions are preprogrammed much like the buttons of a car radio, and when the trigger happens we just hit the button. At work, we're asked to work overtime and we push the button programmed for a deep sigh, a dejected "sure. I can do it …" followed by a low, muttered, "You thoughtless SOB." So much of our behavior is habitual: an automatic response conditioned over time.

But the three Rs allow us to recondition ourselves to be thoughtful about our reaction to a circumstance. We can even make it a conscious action, deliberate and chosen from a place outside the given situation, and have complete mastery over how we feel and act.

It starts by being aware of our emotions and the subsequent reactions those emotions cause. By beginning to notice our feelings and, just as importantly, what leads up to those feelings and subsequent actions, we are able to make a conscious choice about our actions. Thus, the three Rs of God Confidence–realize, reflect, and replace–are just as basic as "readin', 'ritin', and 'rithmatic." See chapter 4, "God Created Bad Drivers," for an example of the whole three Rs process working together. This is such an important concept that I felt it was warranted to go over it again in this chapter.

Realize

The first step in this process is to realize when we are disconnected from source and spirit, or feeling separate from God. This realization will come in the form of a feeling first, then a thought. Sometimes the two—the feeling and thought—are very close together. For example, we're in a heated discussion, and we say something we shouldn't. Typically, the instant the words leave our mouth we have a heavy feeling in the pit of the stomach, a wave of heat rushes to our head, and we know we've made a grave error in terms of the progress of the conversation. In other instances we may have an unskillful experience, and it may take us a very long time to understand that we could have done better and see the other person's viewpoint. We may get the sick feeling but it may linger with us for hours, days, weeks, or sometimes even longer, eating at us with a feeling of unease. It feels as if something is stuck in our craw as it were, before the real thought or knowing happens that says we've done something in a way that was not of our highest being.

In any event, that moment, whether the instant it happens or days later, is, as my Buddhist teacher says, "a moment to celebrate." The Buddhists have a term *shenpa*, which is defined as the moment we are hooked by an unskillful thought or action. That moment—by any name—is marked by a feeling, an emotion. Our job is to become aware of that feeling. When we attune ourselves to that we begin to *realize* an opportunity. It's an opportunity to train ourselves in understanding, feeling, and being in tune with our emotions, and to control what comes next, rather than just riding the emotional roller coaster. Moreover, it's an opportunity to train ourselves to recognize the situations and circumstance that prompt the emotion. I would even go so far as to say that we know in our heart, even before the emotion (mental reaction to a trigger) happens. Thus, a God Confident life is one lived from the heart rather than the head.

Reflect

Reflection is one of the key attributes unique to human beings. It allows us to see how we could do things differently, and what attitudes and circumstances lead to certain behaviors. Reflection is really the component of this practice to focus on, as it is what leads to our behavior. When being challenged in our everyday life, we can look back to see what in our day or our makeup led to the bad feelings. These are the feelings of tightness, the knot in the stomach, the stress, the anger building, and the thoughts of distraction and history that are not specific to the situation. Clearly they are lingering issues that are showing themselves when triggered by an event.

Reflection is a critical element that must be leveraged, but we have to take care so we don't get "caught in the past." Reflection can be an element where we easily get stuck, looking back too long or too far and beating ourselves up. Then we are spinning through how we could have done something differently, and end up replaying the argument or circumstance over and over. I don't think this is productive. All too often, as the saying goes, we look so longingly at the door that has just closed that we miss the others that are opening. So we must be aware of treading a fine line between taking stock of our emotions and the factors that built those emotions, and getting caught up in looking back. We need to reflect to have the necessary information to catch poor emotions and choices and change them in the future, all the while being careful not to spend too much time looking back. Looking in the mirror too long can be hazardous, especially ones that say, "objects in this mirror are closer than they appear," as those have special trapping power. And it is a trap.

When the exercise of refection becomes a job rather than a moment of attention, we've stayed too long. When reflection becomes a recurring topic of conversation with our friends, we've gone beyond reflection and into analysis paralysis, self-doubt, self-flagellation, and even self-loathing. We can easily get caught in either "woe is me" because of my past, or we make it a job to dig into every nook and cranny of our past and clear it all out.

It becomes an exercise of simply learning from our mistakes and not getting caught up in our story. In running, if I want to run faster in my next event, I have to look at past races and determine the things that worked and the things that didn't. However, that is a pretty simple analysis. If I was not able to finish strong, I can look back at the race and see if I started too fast, or look at the training log and see that I didn't do enough long runs. Once I've made that determination, I have to move on and adjust my training and race planning. It is easy to spend time kicking myself about how I know better than to start a race too fast, or how I should have spent the time running and training harder, but none of that effort is going to make me faster and stronger. What will help is doing more long runs, practicing getting comfortable with a good starting pace, and understanding that I have to control how I go out at the beginning of a race. This is a fine line between learning from my mistake and getting caught up in the self-created drama of what could have been.

I want to be very clear that I appreciate the value of looking at our past, of clearing out the elements that no longer serve us, and forgiving those that have wronged us. I understand that this can be a very important practice for moving on. However, I also appreciate that not everyone may need that level of healing, and that regardless of the depth of one's past anguish, there comes a point that you have to decide if you're going to live your life looking back or forward. Basically, you have to make peace with the past and move on. If you don't, you realize one day that years of your life have gone by in a sullen, searching blur. Time goes by and as it does, it has nothing to do with the past but everything to do with how you choose to live the present, which in turn creates your future. And that is why this particular practice is a three-stepper: realize, reflect and replace. We don't linger in reflection but learn what it can show us, and then move on and replace it with something positive that will create a better future.

Replace

This step is simple: Think of something that makes you smile, and use that thought as a replacement for whatever thought you were having when you realized you were getting pissy. It really is all about how you feel, and what you think affects how you feel and act. When you feel off, your behavior corresponds, and likewise when you feel upbeat, your behavior corresponds. So when we catch ourselves feeling crappy (that's what the three Rs are about; understanding how to recognize our feelings before they manifest into behaviors), we replace whatever thoughts we're thinking with something more positive. Thus, when we have the initial feeling, or realize the situation we are experiencing has the history of getting us in a downward spiral, we need to have a higher-order thought at the ready to replace all that constriction and limitation.

The replacement thought can be specific to the situation. For example, the boss brings a problem to you, and rather than being upset that you have to clean up someone else's mess, you think, "I have an opportunity to shine," "I'm the go-to person on the team to take care of these problems," or "it is so awesome that my boss trusts me." Any and all of those thoughts/affirmations are much higher-order thoughts and put you in a position to better deal with the situation.

Not only does the practice work for the specific situation or the task at hand but more importantly, it empowers you with tools to manage the circumstance of controlling your thoughts and emotions. This ability to control and be deliberate about your actions is the significance of the practice. We often forget that in addition to better managing a specific event or situation, this process is exercising us. We are helping ourselves in the moment, and in the longer run we are conditioning our minds to better manage these situations in the future. We are building a process and mental muscle memory that allows us to perform better the next time a triggering event occurs. Just as with a morning run, there are the immediate benefits on getting out in the fresh air, exercising our body to energize the rest of the day, and feeling the aliveness of activity. But there is also the longer-term benefit of the stamina being built and better health and fitness. And we are taking an additional step toward building a habit, which is a practice of health, wholeness, and joy.

So what do we use as replacement thoughts? As noted above, it can be something specific to the situation (I think the greater the specificity, the greater the power of the replacement.) However, specificity may not come easily in the heat of the moment, at least not at first, so I suggest having some generic standbys to go to quickly and easily, such as:

- This situation is an opportunity for me to succeed.
- This situation is the next step I need.
- This situation is exactly the right thing for me at this time.
- This is an opportunity for me to practice what I am learning.
- I am happy, healthy, and whole.
- There is good in this event, I just can't see it now.
- This is an opportunity for me to serve.

As you practice doing more of this replacement, it becomes more natural and easier to do. Subsequently you'll start an upward cycle in the management of thoughts and behaviors. Just as in running, the more you run the better you become. And the more aware you are of how you feel when you run, the better able you are to plan and practice situations, and thus are more successful when struggles arise. For example, when you feel tired during a run, what are the circumstances of that? Is it just a hard run, or did you go out too fast, or is it a mental block? Knowing the answer to why you got tired and being aware of the feeling around that will allow you to correct the process. You can use that knowledge to change your training, and to practice differently. And through the awareness and practicing of awareness you can determine if your changes resulted in better runs. If so, then continue with that technique. If not, refocus your awareness and try something else until you hit the correct formula.

This mental exercise of practicing the three Rs is no different. There is any number of variables that contributes to our feelings in any particular circumstance. It can therefore take time for us to hone in on how we feel, and what variable is related to that feeling, and subsequently the behavior. We then have some measure of trial and error regarding learning how to manage and control that aspect of our being.

But man, have fun with it. Few things feel cooler than catching yourself getting lost in a negative thought pattern and replacing it with something happy, thus pulling out of the tailspin. Then getting to tell yourself, "I did it," and knowing that you were able to make yourself feel and act better. What a joy and victory, and what sweetness in knowing you've just saved yourself what might have been hours, days, or even weeks of being pissy about something. Instead, you nipped it in the bud—and that rocks!

Waking/Slumber Practices

Beginning and ending the day is such a key part of establishing a God Confident life and such a healthy way (physically, emotionally, and spiritually) to be that I'd recommend this as one of the practices you choose first when starting to build your God Confidence. Mary Morrissey says each day is really a lifetime in miniature, with a beginning and an end, and stuff in the middle that can't be done over. With that in mind, what better way to establish a lifelong habit of God Confidence and to establish a process for really living and enjoying each day than by starting and ending each day in spiritual awareness and practice?

There are a number of elements that one can use in a waking and slumber practice, but regardless of what tools or elements one incorporates, the theme is the same. Waking is a time for gratitude, visioning, and preparation. Be grateful for the waking itself and grateful for the abundance of the day to come, where you are planning how the day will go (see "Visioning the Day"), and starting the day from the perspective of God. Slumber is a time for gratitude and reflection on the benefits from the day, the benefits you've given to the world, and an opportunity to take your connection with God and your vision into your dreams.

Here's my waking practice:

When I wake, *before* getting out of bed, or thinking about what time it is, the weather, the run, or whatever, I

- say, "thank you, God, for the waking and the day before me";
- say "thank you for the opportunity to create this day as a benefit for me and all beings I come in contact with";
- say my affirmations (these will be personal, and you can create your own or borrow from others, but whether you borrow from Stuart Smalley or Louise Hay, your theme should be to remind yourself you are a gift, you are happy, healthy, and whole, and you are God Confident); and
- plan the day in the form of prayer and affirmation: outline how things will go, that I'll be joyous and grateful throughout the day; that I'll find the right words at the right times to communicate effectively, and my work will be easy and productive for me, my employer, my clients, and coworkers; that I will have safe travels, and so on. I find the more specific I am the better, particularly if I have a big meeting or significant project needing attention that day. But there are also benefits in the generalities of moving comfortably and confidently through the day, celebrating the abundance of the

day, and being a beneficial presence throughout the day with safety, security, and happiness.

Here's my slumber practice:

- As soon as I get into bed I tense every muscle as tightly as I can for a couple of seconds and then release, focusing on letting go of any and all tension (this can be done two or three times).
- Take a deep, deliberate breath, hold it, and then release it, focusing on letting go of any and all tension (this can be done two or three times).
- Give thanks for the day that has just passed; express gratitude for safety and security; give thanks for the opportunity of the day and for the beneficial presence of myself and others during the day.
- Ask for support in dealing more skillfully with any situations from the day that did not go as well as I would have liked and give thanks for a restful and rejuvenating slumber.
- Then, much like in the waking practice, say my affirmations.
- Engage in deep, concentrated thought about my vision (this is a long-term vision of the life I love living).
- Usually, I fall asleep at some point during this process. Don't despair if you establish a practice and don't get all the way through it. I take that as a sign that my body is ready to rest, my soul is ready to celebrate, and my thoughts are positive and charged with gratitude and good-feeling emotions.

The really critical element of this waking and slumber practice is that you establish a connection with God the first thing in the morning and the last thing at night. Establish a practice, give this time to yourself and to God, and begin to really take note of the changes you see and the difference you feel in your life.

Ray Roberts

See the Little Things

Are there really any little things? Maybe I should say see the things that typically go unnoticed, or that we sometimes take for granted. When I run in the mornings, I am usually greeted with a great moonset and a wonderful sunrise. Both are easy to miss in the rush to get out the door, which, particularly in winter, means donning many layers: a hat, gloves, reflective vest, and headlamp, then getting the dog's leash and vest. Then there is the focus on the run: short speed, tempo, long run—getting your head together for whatever the run holds can be taxing. But it can also be a joyous moment, if we are present.

Being attentive to and aware of the morning routine, consciously doing one thing at a time, feeling the breath and the movements of the body, can help slow it all down. Then you can notice, out the front window, that giant, bright, white orb of the moon lighting the morning landscape, or, the lightly cloud-shrouded orange globe of the sun rising from behind the distant tree limbs. Those views are so cool and can help us remember how small we are yet how big our potential is. Literally and spiritually, a part of us put that moon up there; the very physical makeup of that moon is in each of us, and the joy to *see* it and make meaning of it and find comfort in it is in us.

Many of my mornings start this way. They continue with the sound of the dog's collar jingling in the distance as she trots up the drive and explores what the morning has brought to her. She lingers in the scents of the creatures of the night, the winter's gift of a morning frost, or the summer's harbinger of the heat of the day in the humid dew on every blade of grass. As the run starts, I feel the night's leftover stillness leave the body as the natural fluidity of running takes over and the strides stir the air on my face as we launch into the darkness of the morning. Just as each day holds promise and opportunity, the run provides the same, with the chance to start the day with the appreciation of the little things. The chirp of the birds starting their day and the scurry of nocturnal critters heading to the burrows for their rest provide a good-morning greeting and a reminder of the connectedness of it all: the cycle of night and day and flow of nature, of me in all that is around me.

Regardless of how you start the day, begin to pay attention to all that is around you. Inventory your field of sight, touch, hearing, and smell. Begin to count the different things you notice as you get up, prepare for the day, run your errands, and go to work or school. Really *see* all the things around you and appreciate the natural and greatness in each one. This practice will not only increase your sense of appreciation for those things, but it will begin to train you to be more aware of your world and subsequently more grateful and connected to the all that is.

Laugh/Smile

"Laughter is the best medicine" and "It takes more muscles and effort to frown than smile." Whatever the trite sayings are that we associate with the benefits of laughter, smiling, and joy, the truth of the matter is it's nice to see someone smile. It is fun to hear laughter, and it is contagious. And it is easy to just smile. Sometimes it seems like we work so hard to be jaded. We act as if there is some sort of prize for being the most cynical, that those of us hardened by the realities of the world are in a better position to live and succeed at life.

We often approach life in a vein that says any sort of frivolity is taking time away from hard work. We seem to look at things in zero-sum terms. I can either laugh and smile or be hard and work. What a God Confident life teaches and allows is that even most nose-to-the-grindstone-type folks can (and should) laugh. Lightheartedness and hard work are not mutually exclusive. Smiles are not the exclusive property of the clown. And here again, it is a bit frustrating to feel like you have to defend happiness. But much like affirmations, laughter and smiling are overlooked in their power and function in our lives.

I think too often we feel like there has to be a clear line between work and play, between seriousness and playfulness, between daily life and spirituality. But what if we stopped trying to categorize and segment everything into specific times and activities? What would it look like (and feel like) if we just let things be, and noticed that when we feel good we should smile and laugh regardless of the circumstances? I think we'd find a more natural and easy flow to our lives, and joy would start to be more apparent in our world.

More importantly, we should probably spend more time being aware of when we don't feel so good. And in those moments, we should force ourselves to smile and laugh. We should make a conscious effort to insert smiles throughout the day. I think too many times we feel we have a role to play; a perception that we have to keep up appearances. We want to make sure we seem like people think we should seem.

All too often our judgments about others and ourselves are based off assumptions we leap to because we are scared of the unknown. Or we are scared to *live* in the moment and just deal with situations and circumstances as they arise and as the flow of the world comes to us. To be frank, we make crap up about a situation or circumstance so we can then set up how we should react, do, or be. I wonder how much of the struggle, violence, and dissonance in our world are due to faulty and misguided assumptions about what someone else thought, said, or did, and how it related to us?

We do this because we are not God Confident. We are uncomfortable living in our own skins, and we have to build scenes around all that we do so we can feel we have a sense of control. What would it look like if we didn't do that? We'd be a lot happier, we'd smile at others, and we'd build a repertoire of joy (smiling is contagious too!) We'd laugh about funny things and enjoy the flow of life without the struggle of having to control all that is around us. We'd just smile and laugh and *live*. So smile as if your happiness and your life depends on it, because it does.

Exercise—Mind, Body and Spirit

Our human form houses the experiences we have. Mind, body and spirit are all contributors, so we have to take care and keep the body, mind, and spirit healthy. These components work hand in hand to build our reality and participate in the process of life. To that end, exercise of one is really exercise of all, and we just have to be awake to the opportunities for exercise, and subsequently believe that our activities are going to be exercise for the mind, body, and spirit.

Study after study has consistently validated what regular exercisers have long known: Exercise is good for you. Exercise clearly supports better physical health, but now more evidence is showing that it helps folks feel better, reduces stress, increases mental clarity, reduces the risk of many diseases, and increases longevity. When putting this in a spiritual context, exercise fosters a clarity and focus that strengthens our bond with the infinite.

Run, bike, swim, walk, play a sport, do yoga, ride a horse, garden, whatever—any activity that gets the body in motion also exercises the mind and spirit. Be aware of the opportunity to exercise all components of our human existence. Know that while these physical forms of exercise are focused on the body, the mind and spirit are reaping benefits as well. The proverbial "runners' high," the appreciation of the beauty of the surroundings as you run, the grand plans and visions you build in your mind, all of this is exercising the mind and spirit while the run is exercising the body. If you're playing a sport or running for time, the mental efforts of keeping up with the game or calculating your pace and distance are benefiting your mind.

The final attribute that exercise supports is the practice of doing something regularly. For me, running is not only a physical and mental exercise, but it is a process exercise. In other words, establishing an exercise habit teaches me how to devote time to a thing, how to be diligent in it, and how to enjoy the process of doing a thing. So not only are we supporting our physical and mental health, we are also teaching ourselves and practicing how to go about an activity. This can carry over into our personal and professional lives, making us better able to function in our world.

Read More

There is a saying that the company you keep says a lot about you as a person. I think that is true, but I think too often we take it so literally that we allow those around us to create the kind of person we are. I agree that birds of a feather flock together, and I do all I can to make sure the birds around me are positive. However, I also know there are times when I'll have to deal with and spend time with folks who may not share my same perspective or values. We must deal with this reality.

One of the easiest and most fulfilling things we can do in building a close band of positive and influential like minds is to read. The more we immerse ourselves in reading those that give us guidance, wisdom, and insight, the more we are building our own virtual and mental flock. While I may not know the authors personally, the books (magazines, newspapers, Internet articles) I read give me a glimpse into the lives of the great ones, and give me a conversation with them I might not otherwise have.

So read! Read things that interest and excite you, things that make you think and move you outside your comfort zone. Read things that provide guidance and support for how you want to be and things that inspire you to think and act in a higher manner. Read spiritual works that will help remind you of how to be more God Confident.

Reading allows me to not only formulate new ideas, but also to gain confidence in my understanding of a particular field. And while I may not be able to have a sit-down with Dr. Norman Vincent Peale, I can read *A Guide to Confident Living* and have a glimpse into Peale's thoughts and ideas. Those concepts can assist me in the formulation and expression of my own ideas, and it can be as if Dr. Peale is a buddy of mine who gives me great advice on a daily basis. Reading allows me to expand my range of thought, allows me to strengthen my ideas, and gives me a support process for my day. It has been said that reading the works of the highly enlightened can rub off on you, and I believe it. Reading positive and uplifting books can also help keep your vibration up, especially when you have allowed the events of the day to get to you. It can also help you stay on track with your positive vision for yourself.

Much like running exercises the body and prepares me for a specific type of race, so too does reading exercise the mind and prepare me for a specific type of thinking. Below are just of few of the authors I lean on, and would suggest as good partners in life.

- James Allen—eloquent discussion on thought creating our reality. Specific title: *As a Man Thinketh*.
- Dr. Deepak Chopra—just a myriad of great work. A lot on the perspective of health and spirituality. Specific titles: *Perfect Health, Seven Spiritual Laws of Success, Seven Spiritual Laws of Parenting*.
- Dr. Wayne Dyer—concepts on the power of our thoughts on the world around us, making real what we desire through our thoughts and actions. Specific titles: *The Power of Deliberate Intent, Inspiration*.
- Louise Hay—excellent works on healing your body, mind, and spirit, and how to use affirmations and positive thinking

to create the life you desire. Specific title: *You Can Heal Your Life.*
- Ester and Jerry Hicks—laws of the universe as told to Ester from Abraham, a collective of higher-order spiritual beings. True laws and explanation about how the world works. Specific titles: *The Law of Attraction, Ask and It Is Given.*
- Mary Morrissey—developing a connection to spirit, finding and living your passion. Specific titles: *Building Your Field of Dreams, No Less Than Greatness, Prosperity Plus—A New Way of Living*
- Dr. Norman Vincent Peale—old-school Christianity with a new thought twist on manifesting the life you want to live. Specific titles: *A Guide to Confident Living, The Power of Positive Thinking.*
- Parmahansa Yogananda—a yogi from India who traveled to America and taught an Eastern perspective on how to be one with God. He is also the founder of Self-Realization Fellowship. Specific Titles: *Autobiography of a Yogi, Man's Eternal Quest.*

- Holy texts:
  - the Bible
  - the Quran
  - the Bhagavad-Gita
  - the Tao Te Ching

Others authors of note include Rhonda Byrne, Pema Chodron, Emmet Fox, Byron Katie, Dan Millman, and Neale Donald Walsch.

To summarize this chapter of daily ways, don't forget—with all the planning, practices, and opportunities—to act. You must think it first, but then act upon it. While thinking alone won't do it, it will lead to action. Thinking about God Confidence will start you contemplating more about it, and the more you think about it, the more your thoughts will lead to doing something about it. So think about adopting one or two of the practices listed in this chapter. Try them for at least twenty-one days, which is the minimal amount of time it takes to start a new habit. And most importantly, have fun with the practice. Just as the process of training for a marathon starts with a plan and a few easy runs, so too does the practice of God Confidence start with a couple of daily practices. And as with running, the results may come slowly—but they will come. Notice not just progress toward the end goal, but the small steps you take as well. It is all good stuff, and all forming the basis for better practice and God Confidence.

6

Airy-Fairy versus Joe Six-Pack

'Cause I heard Jesus he drank wine and I bet we'd get along just fine.

—"Heart Like Mine," Miranda Lambert

WHY IS DAILY involvement with spirit a challenge? Because the day is filled with obligations: we need to be somewhere, do something, answer a question, do a job, live life, take care of *xyz*. Particularly in our fast-paced, information-overload world, it is difficult to step back and take a breath—let alone a breath into ourselves, our being, and our God Confidence. With all that modern life seems to demand, how do we reconcile the need to be an average Joe with the need to be an Airy-Fairy?

Airy-Fairy: one who believes in the unknown, acts on intuition/ gut feelings, talks about spirit and God (*gasp*—outside of church), practices spiritual rituals, has a meditation room with an altar, prays at meals/before bed/before waking/throughout the day, and generally exhibits an otherworldly confidence and perspective about the goings on of the world.

Joe Six-Pack: one who has to pay the bills, take care of things, fight the good fight and run the rat race, climb the corporate ladder, and asks, "Do I have to change my life to be God Confident?"

The answer is no, you don't have to change your life to be God Confident, but being God Confident just may change your life!

Whatever your daily routine is, part of God Confidence will allow for reflection. Reflect on the things you do, their impact on yourself and those around you, and (perhaps most importantly) how those activities make you feel. The reflection and the feeling part is how we begin to be aware of our actions and our personal relationship with God. Subsequently, it helps in how we condition ourselves to modify our behavior and improve our personal relationship with God, ourselves, and others.

Building a personal relationship with God would be much easier without the distractions of the world around us, or so we assume. But we can't all become monks, sell all our worldly possessions, and move to a Tibetan monastery. So we are left with the daily grind and finding a way to integrate God Confidence into it. As Jesus said, we must learn to live in the world, but not be of it.

To do that, do you have to change what you do? Such as quit smoking, give up drinking, attend anger-management courses, go to church every Sunday—or whatever behavior modifications you conjure up when you think about establishing a personal relationship with God.

I would say no! As the Miranda Lambert lyrics above note, "I bet he'd understand a heart like mine." God created all that is, including us, but it is up to us to determine our action in all that is. Things in this world are not inherently good or bad; it is our reaction and application of those things that causes a particular outcome that we then characterize as good or bad. A drink every now and then is not inherently bad. However, a drink that keeps us away from our family at dinner, that makes us do things we would not normally do, or that makes us late to work, is a cause for concern, reflection, and an opportunity for behavior modification.

The reasons for our actions are also in need of analysis. Take, for example, the drink that is a part of a dinner party with friends versus the drink that is alone, to take the edge off after a bad day. But what about the drink that is just a single drink versus the drink that leads to too many more? Any time we reflect and see ourselves burying our problems in the bottom of a bottle, or a shopping bag, or a stranger's arms, we have an opportunity for behavior modification.

When it comes to building a God Confident life and reconciling Airy-Fairy with Joe Six-Pack, I view it just as I would any other relationship in our lives. We do things on a daily basis to nurture and build on our personal relationships. So too must we do things in our daily lives that nurture and build on our personal relationship with God. And the reflection on our behavior is the same. When we do things in our daily lives, we reflect and determine whether or not that action was helpful or hurtful to a given relationship. Usually, we get fairly immediate feedback in our human relationships: We make someone mad, or cause them to laugh or cry. All of that is feedback that tells us to either do more or less of a particular action based on our goal in the relationship.

Our emotions provide that same sort of feedback in our personal relationship with God. Did that particular action make us feel good or not, feel closer to God or not? Sometimes though, the signs from the divine—through emotion or other means—are too subtle for us initially. However, just as we learn to take cues from a partner about how they feel without them saying so, we should have as a goal to improve our intuition and relationship with the divine so we are better able to act on those subtle signs from the universe. In any event, we can apply the reaction and feedback from our human personal relationships to guide us in our personal relationship with God. Any behavior that interferes with our relationships with our spouse, kids, significant other, or our friends is going to interfere with our personal relationship with God. This is because God is reflected in all of them.

If we are having problems in our personal relationships, it is a sign that we are disconnected from our relationship with God too. If our friends are riding us about quitting smoking, getting our debt under control, or whatever, it is a good indication that the behavior in question is creating noise in our personal relationship with God too. Sometimes the signs are not so subtle, and we get a harsh reaction from the universe. Let's be intent on seeing the signs in order to avoid being whacked in the head by a big wake-up call.

Think back to the olden days when most writing was done with a pencil and paper. If you made a mistake when writing something, you would erase the mistake and write over it. But the actual mechanics of that process occur in three parts. First, looking back to see if there have been mistakes, like checking our work from our school days, and quality checking for the business folks. We have to go back over the writing to see if we've misspelled anything, used a word out of context, or left words out. This is the first step of the process. If we don't check our work (review our behaviors), we'll never know how we are doing, sometimes we demonstrate a great lack of care about the end result. It is a matter of attentiveness.

The next step involves the eraser. We see that we've erred and need to correct, so we erase what we've written. But we have to understand why we made the mistake, or what caused the error. We have to take care in this step to make sure we erase well and wipe all the little pink rubber and black graphite bits from the page. Not doing this really causes problems; we end up making the page hard to read with the gray smudges all over the paper, or hard to write on with the tiny eraser chunks all over, like tiny potholes to our vehicle the pencil. We must do some clearing of the page and of our minds. And to do that, we have to reflect on the cause of the error (or behavior) and allow it to be cleared from us before we can continue the writing process.

The final step is to write the correct word. Now that we have a clean place to write, we have to know what word we want to write in place of the mistake. Not doing so means that we make the same mistake over and over again. Have you ever had the experience of misspelling the same word a couple of times or writing the word you just erased over again? When that happens you must erase again. You keep doing that over and over, either because you didn't clear the paper well enough or because you keep messing up, and pretty soon you have a page of smudged thoughts and holes where the eraser has worn through the page of paper (and the page of your mind).

So it is imperative to have the correct spelling, the right context, and a more appropriate word to properly convey the idea at the ready.

From a personal perspective, that means one must be devoted to a personal relationship with God and have God Confident thoughts at the ready when the opportunity to erase is at hand. Do you have to change your life? Not necessarily, but you may.

For example: If you've started a meditation practice as one of the daily ways but you're feeling pressed for time, you could just skip it today, knowing you'll get to it tomorrow. However, employing the three Rs you could: realize the feeling of guilt or questioning tone in your mind when you think about skipping. You then reflect on why you're feeling a time pinch. Finally, you replace the harried thoughts of everything on your to-do list with a relaxed smile and the consideration that everything goes much smoother after you take time to meditate. Or you can consider how important it is to take time for yourself. This is a quick and easy three-step process that can literally be done in a couple of seconds and can help you to move the focus back on building your relationship with God.

Getting ahead seems to be at the forefront of our daily activity. The perception seems to be that success is a zero-sum game. I have to win, and that is the only option. I have to beat the person next to me, because there is a limited supply of opportunity. However, I would suggest that we start to work from a concept of abundance and realize that there are a number of opportunities for success both in career and in spirit.

As career aspirants, we have been told to have a clear direction when it comes to building a career. We must understand what the next level of advancement is, and what the requirements are for those positions. And that is really good advice: You must know where you want to go and how to get there. But one must take care to not become overly myopic when it comes to career advancement. Too often we exercise the adage of looking so longingly at a door that has closed that we miss that another has opened. Or we spend all our time focused on getting ahead, competing, and winning at all costs, and we don't even realize there are costs.

From the perspective of running, I have clear goals and a training plan in place to help me reach those goals. But I also have secondary goals that go beyond specific times or events. Additionally, I make sure I find joy in the simple pleasure of running, being out in nature and enjoying the wonder of my world as I run. I enjoy the journey, not just the destination.

Thus, we should realize our definition of success can change. It can and probably should be flexible. It is fine to have a primary focus, but be open to the things that come your way that might not immediately fit your expectations; they may ultimately create a better opportunity. Don't paint yourself into a corner in your urge to compete and get ahead. Allow yourself the perspective of enjoyment, flexibility, and abundance. Additionally, I'd challenge all to add a spiritual component to your definition of success. A daily spiritual presence, and the peace of mind that comes from it, is *not* exclusive of success. If anything, it will help to improve the success in all other aspects of your life. As Jesus said, seek God first, and all (these) things shall be given to you (Matthew 6:33).

All too often we treat life as separate components that must be balanced. Work, family, and hobbies are all distinct and placed on the grand scale to be weighed against one another. In reality, I see those elements as cogs in the machine that is *us*. Some of those cogs are large and turn slowly; others are small and turn quickly. But they all must work in sync with each other. If one gets out of sync with the others and spins too quickly or too slowly, the whole machine can break down. We should also consider that we, not the external world, can control the size and speed of our cogs. It is a dynamic system that changes over time.

Particularly from a male point of view, we've come to see the world as something that must be conquered. Whether it is sports, our jobs, or our family life, there is a feeling of conquest, of winning, and of keeping up and getting ahead. All too often this becomes our driving force. We lose sight and, more importantly, feeling of our spiritual selves and our connection with the flow of the universe when focusing only on the external. While we cannot ignore the external, we can establish a sense of wellbeing with God Confidence. We can develop attentiveness to our internal and external worlds and subsequently work on bettering the external by being attentive to and bettering the internal. When we look at our world, it is measured by largely external criteria: car, job, bank account, body image, who we know, and fashion. All of those items are significant. They are a part of our world and to a certain extent are required to get along in the modern world. *But* those do not have to be the only measures, or even the main measures. God Confidence allows and requests that we focus on internal measures, and supports our evaluation of the external in a nonattached way. We can establish things we'd like to achieve, such as desires and preferences in our external lives, and move calmly and confidently toward those, while we enjoy and live a God Confident life. When those external measures become our only criteria, we lose our connection, and we become controlled not by our spirit but by our measure of the stuff we have. A preference, rather than an attachment or single, threaded focus, allows us to plan, progress, and acquire the things that make us comfortable, without having such an extensive attachment that it consumes and disconnects us.

This dichotomy between an internal focus of spirituality and an external focus of materiality is really not as challenging as it sounds. It is just a matter of focus. It is our focus on God Confidence and our practice that allows us to manage both the internal and external forces. We can take joy in success on both fronts and, most importantly, revel in our awareness of glory being available to us on both the inside and the outside, knowing that, ultimately, the power is within us always and we just have to be willing to be faithful and exercise our God-given capability to express our joy in every instance.

7

I Know These Two Guys ...

Don't let me get me
I'm my own worst enemy
Don't wanna be my friend no more
I wanna be somebody else"

—"Don't Let Me Get Me," Pink

WE ALL HAVE a story. For some of us, it wholly defines our world. For others, it's a reminder of what not to do, and for still others, it is something that pushes us to be better, do better, and enjoy the world around us.

If you feel your story is one you lament about daily and feel you're a hazard to yourself, let me recount the stories of these two guys I know. Hopefully, you can relate to the emotions, process, and thinking that goes into their stories and, more importantly, how they deal with it.

Both men grew up in small, rural towns in southwest Missouri. One young man had what one might consider a challenging childhood. He grew up in a single-parent household, as his father died when he was young. His mother was forced to move back in with her aging mother and two sisters. The home he grew up in was the family farm, and it had received very little care and maintenance over the years to the point that there were leaks in the roof, drafts around all the windows and doors, and no indoor plumbing. I recall the stories of his embarrassment of having to bathe in a large metal tub in the smokehouse that was filled with water heated in a kettle on the wood stove. That stove was also the heat source, so he recounted that bathing in winter was a quick process. He was never able to have friends spend the night, as he didn't want them to experience his daily routine. Living on the farm meant lots of chores and very little money. About the time of his father's death, one of his aunts broke her ankle severely, and so his mom took on her role in keeping the farm running. Even after the aunt was back at home, her injury, his mother's ailing mother, and the aging sisters, meant his mother stayed at home and just worked the farm. To say they were poor was a bit of an understatement.

As the young man grew up he slowly fostered resentment about his lot in life. Why did his father have to die? Why wasn't there more money? Why did he have to work so hard? Why couldn't he have a home that he could be proud of, and have friends over? He had lots of *why me*s, and a determination that he was moving away from it all as soon as he was able to go to college.

While in high school he managed to have friends but always felt like a bit of an outcast and that he needed to cover up some of himself to avoid being exposed. In the back of his mind he feared being exposed as a pretender in the in crowd, even more so than his already fringe affiliation hinted. He was a skinny, pasty little thing, and girls were not a focus, really not an option, so he turned to speech and debate. Fortunately for him, he was pretty good at arguing. He thought it was from all the arguments he had with himself and from the channeling of all his woe and lament. Being pretty good at debate, and ultimately having decent friends, allowed him to endure some of the teasing that naturally comes upon the geek trying to be a part of the cool crowd. Nonetheless, he made it through high school with some modicum of self-esteem.

I recall him telling me stories of his struggles to belong. While he didn't reflect on them as being attempts to belong, it was clear he was hanging out with these people to be a part of something, and was trying to find unique ways to define himself. He simply wanted to be normal, yet unique. He dreamed of being different in a revered, rather than mocked, sort of way. While "normal" for a teen is always a bit skewed, he viewed his circumstances as the boundary of his being and his normalcy.

So while he lived in a house without indoor plumbing, in a household made up exclusively of old to elderly women, participated in speech and debate, was poor, and looked the part of the geek, he strove to be one of the cool kids. He befriended the athletes and well-to-do, talked a good game about girls, played up a class clown role, and participated in student government. He skirted the sidelines of the cool parties and did all the things that someone clinging to circumstances to define themselves does. His experience as he described it to me was one of total external focus and a complete lack of knowing himself and what he really wanted to do with his life. Maybe that is how it is for all teens, but today he seems truly troubled by how much he let the world around him dictate who he was and what he would do.

This other guy I know grew up in a similar rural community in what can only be defined as a limited financial upbringing. However, my friend never relayed to me that he felt any lack in his upbringing. This guy talked about the optimism he felt growing up. At times, he said he felt like he was being put on the spot with the level of responsibility his mother provided, but he said it always worked out. No matter how minor the task or incident, he always felt, perhaps not always consciously, better about himself and more in control of his world.

His mother's optimism extended to all aspects of his life. He often heard phrases like "you can do whatever you want," "you can be whatever you want;, the simple "you can do it," and the occasional "I don't care, you're the one that will have to live with it, not me." While not really significant in any one instance, the culmination was that my friend grew up with a great sense of confidence and control. Perhaps at the time, it was not necessarily a sense of confidence on the surface. It was more of a clear sense of being a part of the world, in the flow of opportunities, and having a clear sense that anything could happen. And that optimistic and confident perspective was not just by happenstance. It was built by the ongoing support of his mother's optimism and his practicing what she preached. It grew into him having control, almost a will, to decide how things should be.

Neither my friend nor his mother knew anything of concepts like positive thinking, cocreation, or deliberate intention. But she, through her faith in God, understood that a higher power existed and that she had ability to tap into it. She made sure my friend knew that and lived it. She always held fast to her confidence that whatever the circumstance may be, she could be positive and upbeat. She knew she could trust in God in a way that always left her in control, and this gave her options greater than you could ever imagine. This basic, core, and overarching theme was the ingredient that fostered my friend's development throughout his life.

The teen years for this young man were easy and carefree, with enjoyment of school and friends. He had a real and positive experience of all that stage in life has to offer. He said he never really worried about being cool or having the right friends. Instead, he felt he was the measure of coolness, so it was not he being cool because of the people he hung out with, but they were cool because they hung out with him.

These two both went on to college and had somewhat similar paths. Both enjoyed the college experience but in varying ways. My first friend enjoyed success in debate and in academics but still struggled to find an identity. Much like his high school experience, he found that identity in an external focus, by fitting in with the cool kids. But over time he came to see some things as bigger than himself and his circumstances, and he started to have a sense and definition of self that was more internally focused.

The other friend enjoyed his successes as well but describes his experience to me as one of almost watching a show he was in versus actually going through it. He felt confident in himself to the point that it almost became a game. He understood the impermanence of that time and wanted to experience it all. His focus had become more decidedly on something bigger. It was an internal focus, not from a selfish perspective, but from the perspective of being in tune to a larger purpose. Circumstances and events of the day were managed and experienced, but were not defining.

As these two described their college experience, it was if they were coming closer together. Friend One was becoming more aware of the bigger picture, and more comfortable taking responsibility for how he felt and dealt with the world around him. Friend Two, while already enjoying that awareness, also understood the importance of being engaged in the external and was feeling more confident in participating and being vulnerable. He started to realize that would lead to greater experience and fulfillment.

As my friends moved from college to the "real" world, they continued to express to me shared experiences and shared perspective. *Hmmm* ... growing up, perhaps? As adults, both men experienced good and bad circumstances. Friend One began to share more feelings of security regardless of circumstance, and decided he should just be. Friend Two continued to live in the moment, but struggled with doing so in the workaday world of trying to get ahead.

Ultimately they both came to spirituality. They both found that in all the activity of the world there is this larger being that is a sanctuary where calm and peace live. They understood they could visit that sanctuary any time, and that ultimately it was not a place that needed to be visited, but just a place that was. They began to live from that place, not in the form of escapism from problems, but as a quiet place inside themselves, a respite, and a source of strength for dealing with the outside world. They had both found a tool set that made sense of the world and brought back the joy and comfort of knowing they were always doing the right thing.

They both shared with me that as adults they were able at times—or at least aware they were trying—to live their lives in a way that allowed them to deal with the everyday in the most extraordinary ways through their thoughts and feelings. The everyday was not measured by the circumstances of the day but by the extraordinary spirituality they were developing.

This story is not really about two different people; it is just one person looking back at the different feelings, emotions, and perspectives they have of life. Actually, this is me—it is my story. It outlines the competing feelings and struggles I went through on my path up to this point.

Actually, it is everyone's story. There are moments when we feel on top of the world and moments when we feel crushed by it. What's the difference? It's not really that we are two different people, but that our God Confidence, our connection with God wanes. When we live in God Confidence, things are fine, and we don't worry about the evaluation of ourselves. We are content and in God Confidence. When God Confidence wanes, we measure ourselves by the standards of the world around us. Invariably, when we begin to judge, no good comes from it, and we begin to harbor ill will toward ourselves.

In today's world, we call that process the level of self-esteem we have. However, when we talk or think about the self, we must define it as two parts, or sides of a coin if you will. One side is the body, and the other side is the spirit. Both are experiencing different perspectives, but both are together and never able to be defined singularly by a circumstance or situation. Another analogy might be an Oreo cookie. There are the two cookie pieces and the stuff in the middle. And boy, do we love to get caught up in that stuff in the middle. So much so that we think that stuff is really what makes us and what holds us together, and without it, or without attachment to it, we think (and fear) that we will fall apart. But if we take the stuff out, we really see more, we see both sides of the cookie. Not two separate pieces, but two wholes. We see both with two sides, one side we saw and one side we didn't, until we took out all the stuff.

The key thing to remember is that spiritual aspect is always with us. It is an innate part of our being, the essence. And while we may go through phases where the only thing we can see is the practical, situational world, we can know that the spirit is right there too, experiencing the same circumstance, just from a different perspective. When we discover that perspective, we have found the open door to God Confidence.

Conclusion

Can'tcha see there'll come a day when it won't matter
Come a day when you'll be gone
All I want is to have my peace of mind.
Take a look ahead, take a look ahead ...

—Peace of Mind, Boston

THE CONCEPT OF God Confidence is simple yet challenging. It is not unique, and it has been around in many forms for all of time. The lyrics to *Peace of Mind* from the rock band Boston's 1976 album *Boston*, capture some key sentiments on the idea of God Confidence. There is the outer: competition, results, climbing the company ladder. There is also the inner: peace of mind, living, and looking ahead and within.

On the one hand, I have only to *be* (be God Confident) and the rest takes care of itself. And, while this may be our divine state and our natural being, it is not, by human nature, easy. Human nature has engrained in us that things are difficult, and life is a competition and a zero-sum game. Isn't it interesting that as humans we require a descriptor for nature to express our concepts about it? Why can't it just be nature? I think because we look to organize as much unnatural thought and behavior into nature as we can, so we have an excuse. It's okay to be negative, as that's just "human nature." It's okay to feel a sense of lack or fear, as that's just "human nature." But is it really? Isn't nature abundant, supremely organized, and flowing effortlessly for the benefit of all beings? If we really thought that way, we'd not need the term "human nature," just "nature" would do. We'd not be able to discount the feelings of lack and disconnection to it just being how it is. Rather, we'd have to understand and accept that those feelings and thoughts are not natural, but are put upon us by our own lack of focus on God and nature.

The adage of "I'll believe it when I see it" holds true. As does the spiritual twist of "You'll see it when you believe it." In any event, we want results, whether it is financial results, job success, weight loss, fitness, or whatever. We are by nature results driven. And, quite frankly, there is nothing wrong with expecting and wanting results. The key is to accept that the timing, nature, and scope of the results are not based on our perceptions, but on source. Also, we must recognize that results come in both internal and external forms. A key concept of God Confidence is that we accept that the results will come as they are supposed to. Our job is to practice, and let the results take care of themselves. This trusting is how we deal with outcomes that are not to our specific liking.

There is no deal making or negotiation here, only doing/being. We do. We practice. We become God Confident and enjoy. The results will come. It may be trite to say that the doing is its own reward, but isn't strengthening your personal relationship with God a pretty nice reward? Isn't finding peace of mind a fine result even though you can't park it in the garage or see it on a bank statement? How many times have we heard or seen that you can't buy peace of mind or happiness? The benefit and the result are inherent in your peace of mind and in God Confidence.

Exploring our God Confidence is much like learning a language, or becoming a better runner. Immersion is the key: daily practice in practical situations. If you have the need to communicate outside your native tongue, you will find a way to make your needs understood, and to understand the communication techniques of others. You'll point, gesture, or draw pictures (and always speak loudly—somehow we think those that speak a language different from us are also deaf).

Just like with language, we have the capacity to learn God Confidence. We may not "speak" God Confidence at this point in time, but we do have the capacity for or the innate knowing of the basis of communication. We may not be a good runner or even consider ourselves a runner, but we have the capacity to run, and to practice running.

Communication with those around us is our natural state (not the human natural state, just natural). It is the natural state of nearly all beings. The source in us is moving to interact with the source in others, as it is the same source. We communicate with language, hand gestures, facial expression, and so on, all to convey a message. Our personal relationship with God is the same way: We communicate all the time, sometimes more skillfully than others. However, the more we practice, the more we immerse ourselves, the easier the communication becomes, the fewer the misunderstandings, and the more pleasant and relaxed the conversations.

Movement is also a state of gratitude and gives life. Running is a form of that movement and a celebration of gratitude. It can be learned and practiced, and the more we practice, the better we become. The better we become the more pleasant and relaxed the running and the life of the runner will be. Being with spirit, and thinking about God are states of gratitude that give life. The Daily Ways is a form of practice that is a celebration of gratitude. It can be practiced and can make your world better, both for yourself and others.

God Confidence does not absolve us of responsibility or right action. Some may think that the idea of just being is a passive state and one that requires nothing of the actor. In reality, just being is a very active state requiring lots of involvement, thought, and practice. God Confidence does, however, absolve us of fear, a fear that limits responsibility and hinders right action. How often have we not done the right thing because, while we knew it was right, we were afraid of what the outcome might be, or felt that doing nothing was easier? Having and being in the flow of God Confidence is a state that dictates the ultimate in responsibility and right action.

It may seem that there is a theme of "no worries," or "whatever will, be will be," and thus we do our own thing in our own little world. But real God Confidence is living in the world, not removing ourselves from it. It is participating in our life (and by default, the lives of those around us) full on, with a joyful, fearless, and confident—God Confident—nature. This way of being forces a consideration of responsibility and right action. Notice I said *consideration,* as it doesn't always happen. We make mistakes, we forget, we try, and we fail. It is all a part of the process of life, but God Confidence gives us the ability to accept, realize, reflect, and replace thoughts and actions with something we think is better. It is a continual opportunity to be, do, and have more: more life, love, abundance, and peace of mind.

Epilogue

Though we travel the world over to find the beautiful, we must carry it with us or we find it not.

—Ralph Waldo Emerson

Beauty is in the eye of the beholder (or to my old college brethren, beauty is in the eye of the beer holder). This adage has been used for years to describe personal taste, individual opinion, and the subjectivity of the world.

In my mind, it also describes the essence of all spirituality: that the power is within us, in you, and God Confidence is ours. It is with us always, and we are the sole determiners of its use and significance. While it may be different for everyone, beauty (spirit, God) is still mine to define. A personal relationship with that divinity, with God, is mine to define. A God Confident life is mine to define, too.

While our turn of phrase about the beer holder gives one a chuckle, it does really get to the heart of the matter, which is that it is all within us. The power to see beauty is ours. The people don't get more attractive; their physical appearance and personality traits don't improve as the night wears on and the alcohol lowers our inhibitions. But an internal process is going on, and while it is done via a chemical means, the change still is happening to us, in us. While I'm not recommending booze as a path to enlightenment, it is illustrative in that we control the way we look at things.

If we think about it, we do it every day without the aid of toxic substances. Things, events, and people all appear different from day to day, based on our mood, feeling, and perceptions. How often do we "notice" someone that has been around us for a while, but for whatever reason now we really see them in a new way? Why does that happen? Because we have the power and the ability to change how we perceive the things around us. The external circumstances are what they are, and in our value judgments, we deem them good or bad (we certainly don't have to make the judgment of good or bad, but for the sake of the discussion, we'll allow the evaluation to demonstrate the point).

So let's take some of that liquid courage and say: 1) we do not really need the liquid courage, and 2) that we will use our spiritual courage, our God Confidence to *decide* to view every external circumstance differently. This is not saying that we should ignore the reality, but rather we choose to think and behave in a way that makes us feel better. We follow a path that allows us to be more supportive of our own interests and of others, and that defines the beauty for us rather than have it be defined by someone else. There is immense power in that control of our view of the world. That power is really the heart of God Confidence and, subsequently, the process of building a personal relationship with God that ultimately translates into living a God Confident life.

And why is it that we all see beauty differently? Quite simply, it is because beauty is actually in each one of us, rather than outside us. I contend that it is a feeling inside us, not sight, sound, touch, or taste that determines beauty. If we really slow down the process of beauty appreciation, we'd notice that the feeling of awe, or inspiration, or joy actually comes *before* the sight or sound that we ultimately attribute to the feeling. In other words, we *feel* beauty before we see it. Our heart and mind work in concert to generate a feeling that we recognize as amazement, or awe, or joy, and we attribute that feeling to the activity of the moment: viewing a sunset, listening to great music, whatever.

In reality, the beauty and awe of a majestic sunrise is actually within us all the time. The feeling actually comes just before the sight or recognition of the sunrise. The sunrise was just a trigger that allowed us to pause for a moment, be in the present moment, and feel the beauty inside us. It's in us all the time, but we have conditioned ourselves that we need some sort of external trigger—an awe-inspiring view, a moving piece of music, or a smiling child—to launch the feeling. In fact, that feeling is always there, and is not the result of these external stimuli, but is inside each and every one of us. So in reality there is no cause and effect between seeing a beautiful sunrise and feeling good. There is only the effect, which is the emotion of the heart in the present moment, and that is in us all the time. God Confidence allows us to harness that effect at all times and in all situations.

Parmahansa Yogananda, founder of Self-Realization Fellowship, talks about meditation as the access point to God, and that the beauty and ecstasy of finding God in mediation allows you to see unlimited inspiring vistas, and feel warm summer breezes and, essentially, feel love and joy at any time. Thus, the power is within us, and "the Kingdom of Heaven is within us." We just have to quiet the mind, allow ourselves to believe that we can do it, and find the beauty within us versus looking outside or expecting that the feeling can only come through external stimulus. Take the time; establish a personal relationship with God and then "see" beauty all the time and in everything, especially in yourself.

I suppose you can treat all of this as a bunch of bunk, or airy-fairy crap that is meaningless and a useless waste of time. But I would ask, what's wrong with taking control of how you feel and act, being responsible for your actions, and knowing that you can move through life with confidence and compassion, and make the world easier and better for you and those around you? Maybe this *is* bunk, and in the end it will make no difference at all.

But when I try to make sense of things in life, I go back to running. Many would say running is bunk, a complete waste of time. Why run when you could be doing other things? It is too time consuming, and has no real benefits. Why not enjoy your time on earth rather than fight an ultimately losing battle with health and age? But I've tried running, and I know that for me, it makes me feel better. I see the change it has made to my body and my overall health. I move easier and more freely, I have more energy, and I have a perspective of practice and accomplishment that builds confidence that carries over into my daily life. The mental benefits of running can't be overlooked: the will to work through some struggle, to keep going when I want to stop, and the clarity that can come during a run.

As 4 Non Blondes sing, "just to get it all out while it's in my head," I run and let it all go out of my head, clear my thoughts, or think great thoughts, and analyze my world—it's my time with nothing else to do. And for many, running is actually fun. Beyond all the mental and physical benefits, folks just enjoy getting outside, seeing nature and the neighborhood, and getting a good sweat. It is therapy. At a minimum, running makes me feel better, so why not do it?

The same is true of establishing a personal relationship with God and building a God Confident life. It may be bunk and may not serve any ultimate purpose—but it may. And, along the way it will make me feel better, be more at ease with the world around me, be in control of my emotions and not bound by the whims of a comical universe. With the practice and the establishment of God Confidence, I have control. Or at least I'm kidding myself into thinking I do. But isn't that all that counts—what I think/feel about my world? I mean, really, I can live from a perspective of lack, that I have to get mine

God Confidence

at whatever cost and the world is against me. Or I can live from a perspective of abundance, that there is enough; I can stop and smell the roses and know that the universe is plotting for my good.

These are two simple orientations toward life; you choose. You can make of these practices whatever you want, but I choose to feel good. At every turn, I choose how I'll react to a situation. Those that assume that our feelings, thoughts, and actions are beyond our control and are bound to a set of options determined by a chaotic and random world are the truly helpless. They aren't playing by the rules of the world, but they are slaves to them. They are not the wise cynics they think they are, not to be fooled or taken advantage of, but rather poor players in the game of life, too afraid of challenge and the opportunity to take action, to take the opportunity to feel better.

Everyone's path is different. I'm confident it is right for each person at the current time, but it is not set in stone. If you don't like the path you're on, you can, and should, choose another. You should not continue on in helpless despair but rather use the tools and the observations in this book to provide an option, an alternative.

Maybe you're fooled, but what's the alternative? Are you going to be better off by being a sad sack, or a cynic, or a hard-ass fighting at the whims of the circumstances of your life? Or are you going to go through life happy, healthy, and whole, with thoughts of greater good, celebrating ideals that are common to all religions of the world and are proven in everything from running to music to art to business—and to *life*? Thousands of years of recorded history, countless personal experiences, the wisdom of the ages, masters, sages, saints, and poets all tell us this is real. Don't be jaded and cocky, but allow yourself guidance and support. Practice and receive the promise that is yours, and live with God Confidence.

Practice does make perfect, or at least it makes us better. So why not enjoy a God Confident life? The only thing you have to lose is a sour attitude, and the only thing you have to gain is up to you. No limits, no floor or entry requirements, and no ceiling or bounds. Your life is to live as you'd like. I like mine God Confident, and I believe you will too.

Final Thoughts

The God who has girded me with strength has opened wide my path. He made my feet like the feet of deer, and set me secure on the heights.

—2 Samuel 22:33–34

A GOOD DEAL OF this was written while running, so God bless ASICS running shoes and a good dog. ASICS is an acronym for the Latin phrase *Anima Sana In Corpore Sano*, which means "sound mind, sound body."

Much like in running with your dog, a personal relationship with God is easy and natural.

Opportunities exist everywhere, every day, to be closer to God. And as we practice we become better, and God Confidence comes more often and naturally, and soon it is a habit and a way of life. Many runners would describe running in the same vein: the more we do it, the better we become and enjoy it. The more we enjoy it, the more we want to do it, and the next thing you know you feel odd when you don't get in that morning run. In running, if you put in the miles, you will be able to run farther. If you do speed work, you'll be able to run faster.

If you put in time with the practices of God Confidence, you'll be more naturally aware, better able to deal with the situations and circumstances in your life, and have an outlook that supports your character, your relationship with God, and polishes every interaction with a luster that will make you smile and go *ahhh*.

I may never be an elite runner, but I have the confidence to know that I'm better than I was. I continue to improve, and I know that I've achieved. With God Confidence, I may not be an elite spiritual teacher (monk, sage, guru, etc.), but I know I'm better than I was before, I continue to get better, and I have achieved more than I could have ever imagined.